CONSULTING FOR SUCCESS

A Guide for Prospective Consultants

David Karlson, Ph.D.

A FIFTY-MINUTE™ SERIES BOOK

CRISP PUBLICATIONS, INC.
Menlo Park, California

CONSULTING FOR SUCCESS
A Guide for Prospective Consultants

David Karlson, Ph.D.

CREDITS
Editor: **Tony Hicks**
Layout and Composition: **Interface Studio**
Cover Design: **Carol Harris**
Artwork: **Ralph Mapson**

Copyright © 1991 by David Karlson, Ph.D.
Printed in the United States of America

English language Crisp books are distributed worldwide. Our major international distributors include:

CANADA: Reid Publishing Ltd., Box 69559—109 Thomas St., Oakville, Ontario Canada L6J 7R4. TEL: (416) 842-4428, FAX: (416) 842-9327

AUSTRALIA: Career Builders, P. O. Box 1051, Springwood, Brisbane, Queensland, Australia 4127. TEL: 841-1061, FAX: 841-1580

NEW ZEALAND: Career Builders, P. O. Box 571, Manurewa, Auckland, New Zealand. TEL: 266-5276, FAX: 266-4152

JAPAN: Phoenix Associates Co., Mizuho Bldg. 2-12-2, Kami Osaki, Shinagawa-Ku, Tokyo 141, Japan. TEL: 3-443-7231, FAX: 3-443-7640

Selected Crisp titles are also available in other languages. Contact International Rights Manager Tim Polk at (800) 442-7477 for more information.

Library of Congress Catalog Card Number 91-72522
Karlson, David, Ph.D.
Consulting for Success
ISBN 1-56052-006-X

This book is printed on recyclable paper with soy ink.

ABOUT THIS BOOK

Consulting For Success has definite goals.

First, this book focuses not so much on how to consult as on *why* you want to become a consultant, and it helps you assess your capability to consult. After reading *Consulting For Success* you will be in a much better position to decide if consulting is for you.

Here is some of what you will learn:

1. How to make the decision whether consulting is to be your next career step—yes or no. You will be able to make a more informed decision when you finish *Consulting For Success*.

2. Essential information about what it takes to be a consultant.

3. A portrayal of the transition process of becoming an independent consultant—going from an employee to a start-up, self-employed consultant.

4. An evaluation of your capabilities as they relate to those required for consulting.

5. A potential savings in time and money as you make an informed decision—reading this book will help you take a look before you leap into consulting.

6. An understanding of the consulting process. Many examples highlight the tasks of the consultant.

After you complete *Consulting For Success*, selected references on the how-to aspects of consulting are provided. These will assist you in your next steps.

ACKNOWLEDGEMENTS

What made this book possible was:

- The consultants and prospective consultants who have worked with me. They are the source of ideas and concepts that inspired this book.

- Nick Dunten of Editors Express, who has been a colleague, friend, and sounding board. He has made a difference in my work. He also provided invaluable editorial and content criticism that shaped the final work.

- Tom Mierzwa of The Catalyst Group, who contributed unselfishly to the concepts and ideas that form the heart of the text. He provided invaluable editorial review and made a major contribution to the case studies.

- Mike Crisp of Crisp Publications, who gave me the opportunity to create a book that attempts to examine consulting from a new and much needed perspective.

- My family, Claire and Matthew and Cinda Davey, who were so encouraging.

- My first client, Dr. Roger Karsk, who inspired my work with consultants.

ABOUT THE AUTHOR

An independent consultant, Dr. David Karlson (principal of Karlson Marketing Communications) enjoys assisting consultants in all aspects of marketing their practices. In addition, he advises those considering a consulting career. He helps them make the transition from being employed to being self-employed, independent consultants.

He also offers a number of products and services, including marketing workshops, consulting seminars, videos, newsletters, and start-up marketing consulting.

His highly acclaimed 50 Minute Series book *Marketing Your Consulting or Professional Services* (Crisp Publications, Menlo Park, CA 1988) has helped thousands of professionals market their firms. It offers a practical approach to marketing from planning to implementation.

The author welcomes your comments and questions. He recognizes that readers can make a significant contribution to later revisions of this book.

For more information about David Karlson's products and consulting services, you can reach him at: Karlson Marketing Communications, 618 Ellsworth Drive, Silver Spring, MD 20910, PH: 301-589-7260, FAX: 301-589-0806.

CONTENTS

INTRODUCTION

The Popularity of Consulting

So you want to become a consultant. Many people are entering consulting ranks. In fact it's one of the fastest-growing professional areas in the economy. Let's examine some of the reasons consulting has become a growth industry, from both the client's perspective and the consultant's. Check ☑ those that apply to you:

☐ **REASON ONE:** The dream of being your own boss. Becoming an independent consultant doesn't take much capital compared to many other start-ups. For instance, in a major metropolitan area it takes $250,000 or more to open almost any small business. Lauching a one-person consulting practice may require only stationery, a phone, business cards, and a personal computer.

☐ **REASON TWO:** The economy is becoming more service oriented and less product oriented. As a result, more service organizations are hiring more consultants.

☐ **REASON THREE:** Workers see their bosses hire consultants to do work that was previously done ''in-house.'' Some professionals are trading places and entering the revolving door—resigning as full-time staffers and returning as part-time consultants!

☐ **REASON FOUR:** It may be in the best interest of organizations to hire consultants: (1) to keep the permanent staff lean and mean and to keep manpower costs down; (2) to address highly specialized problems quickly; (3) to tackle acute business needs that can't wait for staff to find time; (4) to fill in when the short-term nature of projects cannot support an employee indefinitely.

☐ **REASON FIVE:** Periodic manpower shortages in many fields (e.g., electrical engineers) can be satisfied by consultants until demand is met by training or hiring more staff.

☐ **REASON SIX:** Because of technology the need for qualified staff never seems to approach saturation. Where staff can't be hired to keep up with technological change, consultants fill the void.

☐ **REASON SEVEN:** It has become the vogue to be on your own and define your success. You determine what is important, not the organization. Where basic values are at stake, consulting offers the opportunity to become self-sufficient.

THE POPULARITY OF CONSULTING (Continued)

☐ **REASON EIGHT:** Successful entrepreneurship means knowing what clients need and providing it. If the entrepreneurship bug has bitten you, consulting may be the medium for you to offer those much needed services.

☐ **REASON NINE:** Frenzied merger and acquisition practices have resulted in a look-out-for-yourself employee attitude. Professional staffers and line managers are thinking differently about their futures within the organization. With less job security, the risk associated with becoming a consultant appears more reasonable.

☐ **REASON TEN:** The international community is opening up opportunities for consulting as more and more interest is focused on the global community and its problems.

☐ **REASON ELEVEN:** Consulting can serve as an escape from the doldrums of organizational life. Many employees walk away from their organizations to join the ranks of consulting at midlife, a time when financial risks can be taken with greater confidence.

☐ **REASON TWELVE:** Increased government rules and regulations require someone to help with interpretation and compliance. Every time a new rule or regulation is enacted, an expert is needed—a consultant.

☐ **REASON THIRTEEN:** The information revolution—the advance of knowledge—is happening at a pace that makes it impossible for many to keep up. Consultants are hired to ''keep up'' for their clients.

☐ **REASON FOURTEEN:** It can be enjoyable to be a consultant. Not only is it fun, it can be financially rewarding as well.

☐ **REASON FIFTEEN:** Professionals are seeking a greater challenge in their careers, and an opportunity for professional and personal growth.

☐ **REASON SIXTEEN:** Professionals often become dissatisfied with the lack of opportunity and creativity in their organizational jobs.

WHAT DO YOU THINK?

Why do you think consulting and the use of consultants has become so popular?

How many of the reasons listed did you check? _____

Are there reasons that were not covered that apply to your unique situation? If so, write them here:

_____

_____

_____

_____

_____

The reasons for the growth of consulting may or may not support your decision to become a consultant.

P A R T

1

What Is Consulting?

MORE THAN A JOB—A CAREER!

What is this career called consulting all about? What makes consulting unique?

Take a minute and define what consulting means to you. Write your answers in the space provided.

To me consulting is: _____

_____

_____

_____

_____

_____

It seems that consulting is perceived differently by each individual. This may be because it is different from more traditional careers. Here are some of the most common characteristics of the consulting profession.

1. It is a profession, with professional status and standards.

2. Consulting is a service business. Consultants provide a variety of services.

3. It is characterized by unique client relationships. That is, clients often participate in the work and can affect the outcome. Therefore, management of the client relationship is important in order to be an effective consultant.

4. Consultants are a body of highly skilled professionals with dissimilar backgrounds—unlike all the traditional professions, such as law or medicine.

5. Consultants, regardless of background, are usually perceived as outsiders working on the inside.

It is important to understand the nature of the consulting profession. It differs from what you may have experienced as a traditional employee. If you are clear about this profession, its nature and purpose, you will be in a stronger position for making the transition to independent consultant.

CONSULTING WORK: UNIQUE OR COMMONPLACE?

Now that we have examined consulting as a field, let's look at the work consultants do.

From what you now know, describe the nature of consulting work. What do you think consultants do? Write your answer.

To me consulting work is _____

_____

_____

_____

Consulting work is different from an eight-to-five job. Here are some of the ways consulting work can be characterized.

1. The work can range from routine grind-it-out projects to providing one-time solutions to problems. You may have to prove yourself to your client with a routine project before the more challenging work comes.

2. Problems and needs are often defined by the client, while the consultant participates only in the solution.

3. The work often has specific objectives and expected results that are beyond the control of the consultant. You have to be realistic about what you can accomplish.

4. Ideally, consulting work involves a process: the problem is defined, alternative solutions are considered, a solution is selected and implemented, an evaluation is conducted, the results are analyzed, and follow-up requirements are specified. However, your client may cut corners for speed or cost control.

5. Consulting work is idea driven. This makes it easy to give away the work—that is, your ideas. A common pitfall of the new consultant is to demonstrate capability by giving too many ideas or solutions for nothing—a classic giveaway. Many prospective clients will pick your brains if you allow them. Consultants must say enough to make prospects want to hire them—just enough! You need to know when you have said enough.

6. Consulting is like a game. To win you must learn how to avoid giving away valuable ideas, while at the same time providing a sampling of what's to come. You lose if you give too much away, you win if you give just enough to convince the prospective client to hire you.

7. Consulting involved doing work for many organizations. Consultants have many bosses, not just one!

8. Consulting is very political and sometimes threatening, since much of what the consultant does results in change. Change may be resisted by some people in an organization.

Why Not Talk To a Consultant?

To get some first-hand information, why not talk to a consultant in the field you are considering? Professionals are usually happy to share their views and experiences.

There are professional organizations for consultants. Find out about their meetings and attend with the question in mind: Is consulting for me?

Plan to talk to the following consultants. Write down their names and what they do:

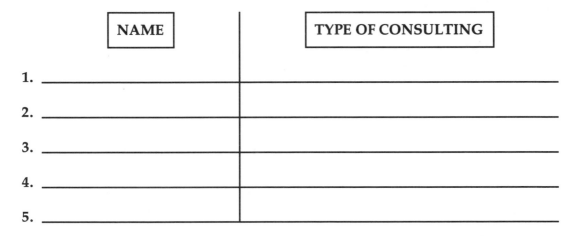

NAME	TYPE OF CONSULTING
1.	
2.	
3.	
4.	
5.	

THE OUTSIDER WHO WORKS ON THE INSIDE!

After talking to several consultants, you can now describe a consultant. Just what is a consultant? Write your answer in the space provided.

To me a consultant is someone who _____

_____

_____

What do other people think a consultant is? Someone who makes a lot of money, someone who is an expert, someone who is in control of their work) Write your answer in the space provided.

As far as I know, people generally think a consultant is _____

_____

_____

Consultants are seen differently by different people. What is important is to define clearly who and what you are as a consultant. To help you do this, look at the following definition.

> A consultant is a professional who possesses skills that are valued and needed by clients. Clients will pay the consultant for those skills that help the client achieve his or her goals.

Does your definition of a consultant line up? Go back and adjust your definition until you are satisfied and understand just how you fit into consulting.

What are some of the misconceptions you or others may have had about consultants?

Describe them here:

1. _____

2. _____

3. _____

4. _____

A CONSULTANT'S MANY ROLES

What confuses people most about consultants is the variety of roles they can play. Listed below are some of those roles. Check ☑ those you plan to play. Can you play them all?

☐ Problem solver: identify the problem and recommend solutions. ____

☐ Idea person: creative methods and approaches to get the job done; the creative source for new ideas. ____

☐ Devil's advocate: the outsider who will challenge the insider approach. ____

☐ Expert: the one that clients turn to when they can't figure something out themselves. ____

☐ Hatchet person: the one who gets rid of an approach or method. ____

☐ Task master: gets the job done with single-minded purpose. ____

☐ Processor: brings a suggestion to the table and seeks consensus. ____

☐ Outsider: brings a fresh, unbiased view to the table; able to see the forest from the trees. ____

☐ Implementer: responsible for installing a new method or system. ____

☐ Catalyst: the change agent who gets things moving in the direction the client wants. ____

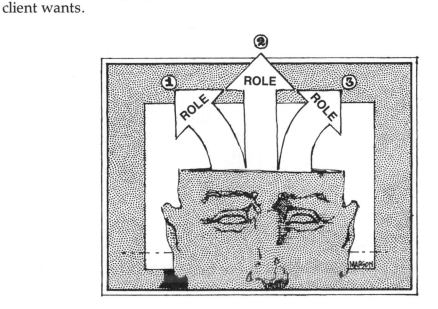

A CONSULTANT'S MANY ROLES (Continued)

Now look again at the roles you checked—the roles you want to play as a consultant. Rank the roles in the order that you would prefer to play them, with 1 being your favorite. Write the numbers in the spaces provided.

Now describe a typical work day you would love to experience. Be detailed. Use the following questions as a guide. Write your answers in the spaces provided.

What time would you get up in the morning? _____

Who would you call? _____

What tasks would you be working on? _____

Who would you be doing it for? _____

Where would you be working (at home, at an office, out of town)? _____

_____

When would you be doing the work? _____

What rewards would you want? _____

_____

_____

What would make you happy as you are working? _____

_____

What role(s) would you play? _____

_____

_____

_____

_____

_____

PART

2

The Successful
Consultant

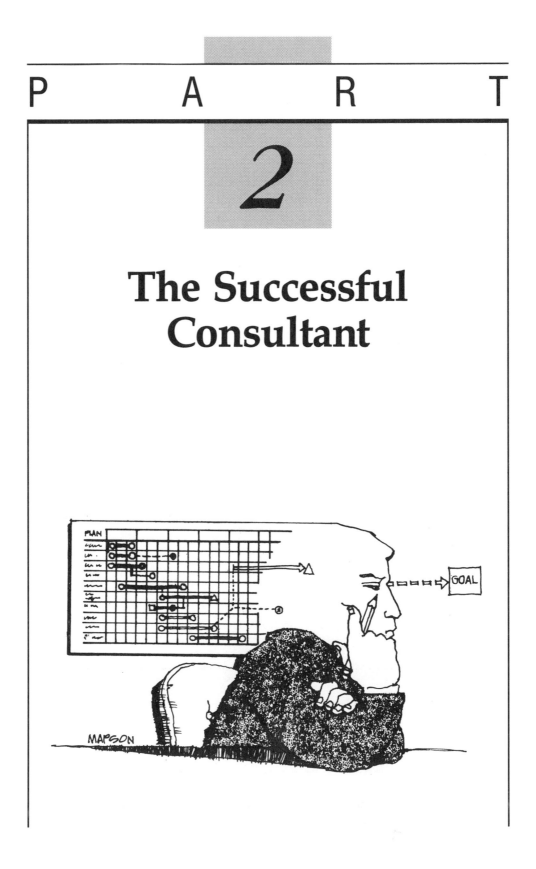

WHY DO YOU WANT TO BECOME A CONSULTANT?

It is important to understand your motivation to become an independent consultant. It will have a major impact on your success—on your ability to establish a consulting practice.

Write down your reason for wanting to become an independent consultant. Be candid with yourself. I want to become an independent consultant because:

_____

_____

_____

Here are some of the most common reasons people have become consultants. Check ☑ all those that apply to you.

☐ **1.** Fame: You want to get the credit for being able to do something better than anyone else.

☐ **2.** Fortune: You want to make lots of money, and you heard that consultants get large fees.

☐ **3.** Reactionary: You're sick of working for someone else and not getting recognition or reward.

☐ **4.** Disgust: You're tired of company politics that reward personalities not performance.

☐ **5.** Entrepreneurial spirit: You dream of being your own boss and calling all the shots.

☐ **6.** Retiring: You want to keep active after retiring—and what better way than to consult?

☐ **7.** Fear of getting laid off: You want to keep one step ahead, so you want to go ahead and start a consulting practice.

☐ **8.** Cashing in on skills: You have all this knowledge and experience—why not get paid what you're really worth?

☐ **9.** Merger or acquisition mania: Your organizational identity is lost and you may lose your identity, too, so you want to get out while the going is good.

☐ **10.** Others that you wrote down: _____

_____

WHY DO YOU WANT TO BECOME A CONSULTANT? (Continued)

From the list on page 15, how many reasons did you check? _____

Which one(s) are your primary motivation for becoming an independent consultant? Number(s) _____

Once you've identified your motivations for wanting to become a consultant, it's up to you to evaluate them. No one knows better than you what works for you in tackling new opportunities.

As you assess your motivation, remember that decisions based on emotion rather than intellect often backfire. Making it through start-up is difficult. To sustain you through this period, your motivation to become a consultant is like a foundation.

Reassess your reasons for becoming an independent consultant. Ask yourself if they are sufficient to carry you through start-up and on to a satisfying career. Write your assessment here:

_____

_____

_____

WHAT IT TAKES TO BE SUCCESSFUL?

Independent consultants work principally on their own. Certain personal characteristics are required. What personal characteristics do you think are required for success as a consultant? List them in the spaces provided.

I think a successful consultant must be:

_____   _____   _____

_____   _____   _____

_____   _____   _____

_____   _____   _____

_____   _____   _____

PERSONAL CHARACTERISTICS OF SUCCESSFUL CONSULTANTS

Below are the personal characteristics that most people agree are required for success as an independent consultant. Check ☑ those that characterize you.

☐ Driven: the singlemindedness to be successful at what you do.

☐ Ambitious: the desire to be successful and to get ahead.

☐ Energetic: the inner resources to stay at it until you get it done.

☐ Self-confident: the attitude that you can do it!

☐ Persevering: the ability to stick to it until you accomplish your goals.

☐ Risk taking: the willingness to attempt new challenges without guaranteed outcomes.

☐ Self-starting: making things happen on your own—without the help of others.

☐ Committed: having a vision and goals that you stick to.

☐ Tough hide: ability to take rejection and come back for more until you get what you want.

☐ Competitive: eager to compete for business and able to enjoy the chase.

☐ Imaginative: able to dream up innovative solutions to unique and perplexing problems.

☐ Assertive: willing to step forth and be counted as well as to be acknowledged.

☐ Communicative: able to speak publicly and write effectively.

☐ Resilient: the ability to recover from failure or disappointment.

☐ Positive: able to take criticism of ideas, develop alternatives, and move on without being defensive.

☐ Detail oriented: no detail is too small to ignore.

☐ Others that you listed: _____

_____

PERSONAL CHARACTERISTICS OF SUCCESSFUL CONSULTANTS (Continued)

How many characteristics did you check? _____

If you checked less than *half* of the personal characteristics on page 20, you should consider how to develop those personal characteristics that you need to strengthen. For example:

- If you do not see yourself as assertive, how do you plan to develop the assertive behavior that is generally required of a consultant?

- If you are not a resilient person, how will you deal with the rejection that consultants often experience?

- If you are now a team player, how will you acquire the self-starter characteristics essential for an independent consultant?

- If you are hesitant to take risks, how will you develop the risk-taking behavior often demanded of consultants?

When you are an independent consultant, all the above personal characteristics will be called upon at one time or another. Once you are a consultant, personal characteristics which may have been latent, may surface and serve you well. However, inventorying them now, and spotting potential shortfalls, will improve your chances for success.

Review all those personal characteristics that you did *not* check from the above list, and plan how you will strengthen each of them. Write your strengthening plans in the spaces below.

Personal Characteristic I Need to Strengthen	Strengthening Plan
e.g., Communicative	Join Toastmasters Club
_____	_____
_____	_____
_____	_____
_____	_____
_____	_____
_____	_____

CONSULTANT SKILLS

To succeed in running a business as an independent consultant, certain skills are required. What specific skills do you think are required to make it as a consultant? List them in the spaces provided.

_____   _____

_____   _____

_____   _____

_____   _____

_____   _____

_____   _____

_____   _____

_____   _____

_____   _____

On the next page is a consultant skills audit. It lists the specific skills that most independent consultants agree are required for success. Use the audit to measure your skill level. It will help you develop greater proficiency in particular skills.

CONSULTANT SKILLS AUDIT

Circle the number that best describes your present skill level.

---

1 = **No knowledge or skills**

3 = **Average skills**

5 = **Excellent knowledge or skills**

Marketing: knowledge of how to get clients that will sustain your practice—selling yourself

        1   3   5

Financial: understanding balance sheets, capital purchasing, how to secure lines of credit, how to develop business plans, and how to manage cash flow

        1   3   5

New service development: coming up with ideas about new services that clients need—research and development

        1   3   5

Service delivery: all aspects of actually providing services to clients once they have contracted with you

        1   3   5

Legal and tax matters: understanding all matters pertaining to taxes and legal issues such as liability

        1   3   5

CEO/management: ability to establish vision for your practice and to guide yourself to achieving your goals

        1   3   5

Interpersonal: ability to manage clients and work effectively within complex organizations as an outsider

        1   3   5

CONSULTANT SKILLS (Continued)

Now analyze your responses. What areas represent your greatest strengths? List them:

_____

_____

_____

How might you capitalize on these areas of strength? For example, if you are good at selling your services, plan to emphasize marketing during start-up. Write down your plan to make the best use of your strengths.

I plan to _____

_____

_____

In what areas are you weakest and need to acquire new skills? List them:

_____

_____

_____

How do you plan to strengthen the weak areas? For example a weakness in marketing could be strengthened by taking a seminar, reading how-to books, or hiring a marketing coach. Write your strengthening program in the spaces below.

Skills I Need to Strengthen   **Strengthening Program**

_____   _____

_____   _____

_____   _____

Comment: Most start-up consultants are strong in service delivery. Most are weak in marketing. So unless you act to strengthen marketing, you may be ''All dressed up with nowhere to go!''

PART

3

Lifestyle of the Consultant

MYTH VERSUS REALITY

How do consultants work and live? Rather than generalize, let's examine a consultant's lifestyle with start-up requirements in mind. The goal of this section is to give a broad overview of what you are about to get into!

Most consultants in start-up report they had a longer work day than in a more traditional job. The reason mainly cited was the tremendous number of tasks required of them. These include:

1. Marketing your practice

2. Doing the actual consulting work

3. Extra effort to do things that you are not always proficient at—such as typing proposals

4. Time-consuming maintenance tasks, such as bookkeeping and billing

5. Continual interruptions, especially phone calls

6. Adapting to working alone

7. Becoming disciplined to self-start and manage time well

8. Staying clear on what your practice is about, and not getting distracted when other opportunities arise

To be effective, you have to be good at juggling severals tasks at once—especially since you are the only juggler! (See *Personal Time Management*, Crisp Publications—a book that will help you gain control of your time.)

How do you plan to deal with your workday? How will you become a good juggler?

I plan to _____

_____

_____

Recommendations for start-ups:

1. Make every effort to manage your time well. It's your most valuable resource.

2. Plan your day, week, and month—and follow your plan.

UNDERSTANDING YOUR SALES CYCLE

Discouragement can set in if you don't recognize the time required for an entire sales cycle. A sales cycle is the time required to actually receive income. It always takes longer than you think to get a regular flow of cash.

The amount of time required to produce income varies greatly among start-up consultants. Knowing your sales cycle can help you deal with the pressures of start-up. You can avoid financial instability by paying close attention to your sales cycle.

Depending on your type of consulting practice, it usually takes time (sometimes years) to produce sufficient income. The pie chart below shows the various aspects of the sales cycle. In the example, it took 43 weeks to produce income.

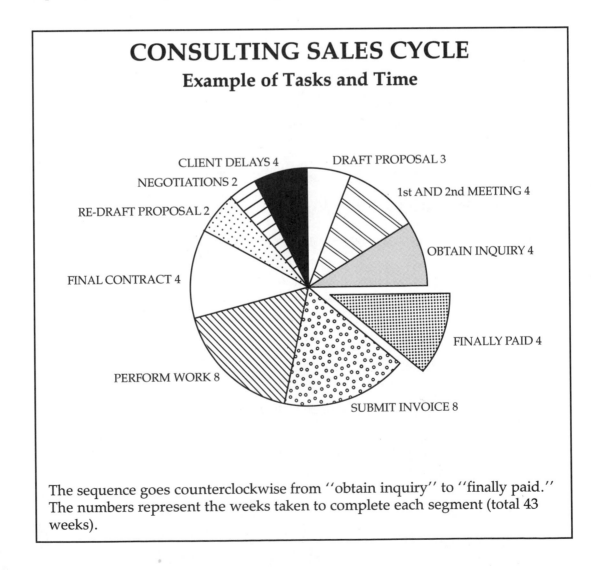

CONSULTING SALES CYCLE
Example of Tasks and Time

CLIENT DELAYS 4 — DRAFT PROPOSAL 3 — 1st AND 2nd MEETING 4 — NEGOTIATIONS 2 — RE-DRAFT PROPOSAL 2 — OBTAIN INQUIRY 4 — FINAL CONTRACT 4 — FINALLY PAID 4 — PERFORM WORK 8 — SUBMIT INVOICE 8

The sequence goes counterclockwise from ''obtain inquiry'' to ''finally paid.'' The numbers represent the weeks taken to complete each segment (total 43 weeks).

DESCRIBE YOUR SALES CYCLE

Now describe your sales cycle—from when you try to generate inquiries to when you get paid for professional services rendered. Write the major steps in the spaces provided.

Major Steps	Weeks to Complete Each Step
1. _____	_____
2. _____	_____
3. _____	_____
4. _____	_____
5. _____	_____
6. _____	_____
7. _____	_____
8. _____	_____
9. _____	_____
10. _____	_____
Total Weeks (equals the length of the sales cycle)	_____

Recommendations for start-ups:

1. Income is irregular, so plan cash flow carefully.

2. It always takes longer to get paid than you expect, so allow more time for payment.

3. Give clients an incentive to pay early.

4. Know your sales cycle intimately.

WHAT ABOUT LEISURE AND VACATIONS?

A commonly held myth is that leisure time will be dramatically reduced, and you won't have vacations at all. That's true—but only if you work hard instead of working smart.

Working smart means taking care of yourself so you can withstand the pressures of being on your own. The demands of self-employment are tremendous compared to being a company person. If you work smart (manage your time well, have a clear purpose and mission, and don't get distracted), you will be able to make time to get recharged. Leisure activity can be your source of regular weekly recharging.

On the other hand, working hard means using up energy without recharging your batteries. The greatest cause for burnout and stress-related conditions is too much hard work and not enough leisure.

Write your recharging plans in the spaces below.

I plan to recharge my batteries on a weekly basis by doing the following:

_____

Each month, I plan to recharge by doing the following:

_____

Each year, I plan to take a much deserved vacation for a major recharge. This year I am planning to:

_____

Recommendations for start-ups:

1. Exercise regularly.

2. Plan vacations, especially long weekends, that get you out of the house and office.

(See *Personal Wellness*, Crisp Publications. It will provide you with all the information you need to put together a wellness plan. It can be ordered using the form in the back of this book.)

WORKING ALONE

As an independent consultant, you generally work alone. This is in shart contrast to working in an organization as a team player. Many consultants in start-up miss the team atmosphere, especially the energy that comes from working with others.

To avoid the isolation syndrome, it's wise to form alliances with other independents—who also want and need the energy that comes from testing your ideas.

In the space below, write the names of some people you plan to form support relationships with:

_____   _____

_____   _____

_____   _____

_____   _____

_____   _____

_____   _____

_____   _____

_____   _____

Recommendations for start-ups:

1. Find a mentor, someone who is or has been a successful consultant.

2. Develop a buddy system for feedback on your plans.

3. Form an informal "board of directors," made up all types of individuals who can give you candid feedback on your practice.

THE BUCK STOPS HERE!

As an independent, you are now responsible for doing all the work. From the smallest task to the largest. From the least important to the most important. What a change from the years of learning how to delegate!

All the tasks are important if the work is to get done. No task is too small or unimportant. You are chief cook and bottle washer. Are you ready for that kind of pressure in your day-to-day work?

Ready ☐   **Not Ready** ☐

Recommendations for start-ups:

1. Do small, less important tasks when you don't feel like working at all.

2. Do the bigger tasks during your high-energy periods. Break these tasks down into subtasks, so you don't become overwhelmed.

3. Create checklists of all the tasks that need to be done. Categorize tasks according to their importance.

PART

4

Making the Transition

FROM EMPLOYED TO SELF-EMPLOYED

There are many ways to make the transition to being an independent consultant. In fact, each transition story is unique. In this part of the book, a number of transition case studies are presented. You may see one that represents the way *you* will go about making the transition successfully.

THE ENTREPRENEUR   *CASE STUDY NO. 1*

Jody had earned a unique education in international affairs, and was trying to develop a new line of business for a large company where he worked full-time. Often frustrated, he would play out various marketing strategies, but seldom ended up with the critical mass of new business it took to support a business unit in this large company.

He was passionate about the intercultural aspects of international work, but couldn't seeem to land enough work to satisfy the overhead requirements which the company imposed.

Deciding that the content of his work was more important than the (temporary) security found in full-time employment, he proposed that the company take him on as a consultant in his area of international expertise. By selling the company on the value of having his expertise available to them at a much lower overhead, he was convincing in his cost-effectiveness argument.

The benefits to him were significant. He had a relatively secure base of operations, the flexibility to chase new business, and an ongoing client with whom he could build a consulting track record.

THE FINANCIAL BARRIER

The need for regular income often impedes the transition to becoming a consultant, since most consultants initially suffer from poor cash flow. The following methods will help you control expenses and maximize income.

MINIMIZE EXPENSES

Several months prior to becoming self-employed, begin to minimize all expenditures. Begin to tighten your belt on spending by scrutinizing *all* expenses, including cars, vacations, clothes, furniture, eating out—anything you can do without. Make a clear distinction between wants and needs. Controlling expenses helps you to minimize the income you need, to survive during the start-up period.

Itemize expenses that you can *eliminate* in the next six months. (Study your checkbook register and credit card statements to see expense patterns.) Write them down:

Expense	Amount
e.g., furniture	$2,000
new appliance	1,000
_____	_____
_____	_____
_____	_____
Total expenses eliminated for the next six months	$ _____

MAXIMIZE INCOME

Several months prior to making your transition, anticipate your income. Determine ways you can *make extra income*. Are there extra projects for your current employer that need to be done? How about overtime? Are there associates who might need your services? Write down your sources of extra income:

Income	Amount
e.g., overtime	$1,000 monthly
aid in computer project	500 monthly
_____	_____
_____	_____
_____	_____
Total additional income for the next six months	$ _____

THE PART-TIMER   *CASE STUDY NO. 2*

Joan had worked for a trade association for several years. Prior to this job, she had served in a variety of marketing-related roles for other organizations. She had accumulated an important mix of skills.

Several events in her life caused her to reexamine her pattern of full-time employment. Her daughter had just begun a new typesetting and desktop publishing business. Her son had decided to leave the family landscaping business to begin a career as an accountant. Her husband had reached the pinnacle of his career, and was thinking of phasing down his efforts and retiring.

Joan saw an opportunity to play a role in assisting the family's business ventures, build a credible experience base as a consultant, and secure a greater degree of personal flexibility. She proposed cutting back to a three-day-week to the association she worked for.

She proposed this arrangement after checking that a junior data entry person would be available to train and groom to gradually take over the responsibilities Joan held. This arrangement allowed Joan to transition into the consulting world, and allowed the association to tap her considerable "institutional memory" and the goodwill she had built up with association members.

DEVELOP YOUR TRANSITION BUDGET

Now that you are looking differently at income and expenses, it is extremely important to know exactly how much money you need to live on for six months once you leave your current employer. In the space below, write your transition budget—first the expenses you must pay, and then the income you can count on.

EXPENSES	Monthly Amount	Total for Six Months
Food		
Rent or mortgage		
Car payment		
Insurance:		
car		
disability		
house		
life		
medical		
liability		
other: _____		
Child care		
Medical and dental		
School tuition		
Other expenses (list them):		
TOTAL EXPENSES		

INCOME	Monthly Amount	Total for Six Months
Salary		
Additional income		
Separation pay		
Retirement pay		
Investments and interest income		
Consulting fees:		
Other income (list the sources):		
TOTAL INCOME		

Now compare the expense and income totals. Will you be in the black or the red over the six-month transition period?

THE DREAMER

Frank was a physicist with a major R&D consulting firm supporting NASA's space station project. Daily, he and his work colleagues would speculate on various small-scale entrepreneurial ventures which might spin off from the high-technology project they were working on. In their own way, they had done a lot of strategic planning and market analysis for a variety of consulting roles without ever realizing it.

During his early professional career, Frank had not written many articles for technical publications, as many of his peers had done. Now, however, he had enrolled in a master's-level university program in the evenings, and recognized he still had the intellectual curiosity to learn about new technological trends and how they presented business opportunities. As he worked his way through this educational ''re-tread'' program, he found that he consistently did study projects that played out his daydreams about using the scientific expertise he'd learned in some entrepreneurial way.

Frank was no venture capitalist. His earnings as an employee were good by professional standards, but nowhere near what it would take to launch a product-based venture. He hadn't let go of his dream to be involved with high technology, though. So, inventorying all his professional connections, he began to construct a series of consulting roles that he would play. By laying out a deliberate plan for the transition from employee to consultant, he built a financial cushion for himself for what he expected to be a slow start-up period of six months or so. During this transition period, he took every opportunity to express his intention to become an expert consultant at some time in the future. In particular, he contacted all the firms he'd worked for in the past.

Fortunately for Frank, his self-promotion campaign was successful. At a time when his space station project began to have funding cutbacks, he had positioned himself to take on several small-scale consulting assignments that emerged from one of his former employers. He left on good terms and kept his options open to return to his firm as a consultant when they might need him.

THE LACK-OF-CLIENTS BARRIER

The sales cycle for gaining an initial client base may take too long, impeding the transition to a full-time practice. Gaining clients immediately makes for the most painless transition. Common methods for overcoming the lack-of-clients barrier involve gaining transitional clients—and transitional income. Here are some of those methods.

1. *Current employer becomes your first major client.*   One of the most common methods of making the transition is to set the stage for your current employer to hire you as a consultant on a part-time basis. To employ this strategy, you will have to lay the groundwork early and be creative about what you can do. Point out the benefits to the employer of hiring you in an interim capacity even while they look to replace you. Don't forget the many advantages you offer: for example, you are completely trained and able to make an immediate contribution. (See Case Study No. 1, The Entrepreneur.)

2. *Current employer lets you work part-time.*   This allows a base income while you are cultivating clients with the rest of your time. It affords a beautiful opportunity for you and allows your employer extra time to replace you. You gain, and so does your employer. You may also maintain employee benefits during transition. (See Case Study No. 2, The Part-timer.)

3. *A former employer offers the opportunity to serve as a consultant.*   Past employers often need help in areas in which you can make an immediate contribution. Let former employers know of your intentions as early as possible, since they may not need you immediately. (See Case Study No. 3, The Dreamer.)

4. *Expand your network six months before leaving your current job.*   By becoming active in professional associations, you can network and confidentially find out who might need your help, especially for part-time and/or consulting work. Begin by finding all the professional organizations you might join and when each one meets. (See Case Study No. 4, The Planner.)

5. *Begin looking for consulting work now.*   If you know the services you want to provide, look for immediate opportunities to begin your consulting practice. As a start, list all the people you know professionally—your network. Systematically contact each person and inform them that you are addressing problems in their field. Ask for referrals—they may know others who might be interested in your services. (See Case Study No. 5, The Jump Starter.)

Which approach will you take? Rank them in the order that seems most appropriate for your situation:

——————, ——————, ——————, ——————, ——————.

THE PLANNER   *CASE STUDY NO. 4*

Janet had worked in the training department of a large metropolitan newspaper for almost six years. For more than a year, she had considered hanging her shingle out as a training consultant, to realize her dream of independence and flexibility.

Looking ahead six months, she set a target date for her break from the newspaper and establishment of her consulting service. During that time she networked with others in her field, conveying the message that soon she would be in business for herself, and seeking to identify potential consulting work.

She used this planning period to put her own house in order as well. She took several courses in accounting, marketing, and communication to enhance her ability to sell herself as a consultant. She also got herself several speaking assignments in locations where she felt there were likely clients.

When the time came for her move, she was ready. She had timed her entry into the field to match with the fiscal-year budget decisions about training services, and had already sold several clients on the value of her services.

She also self-financed her business with $11,500 that she had set aside. She used this money to buy a computer, a laser printer, a fax machine, an overhead projector, a slide projector, and a state-of-the-art telephone answering device.

FEAR OF FAILURE

Making changes usually involves taking risks—from calculated risks to flying by the seat of the pants. Fear of risk can emotionally immobilize you and stop your forward momentum, to the extent that you never make the transition to self-employment. You need to learn how to take reasonable risks.

Remember:

1. Professional growth usually requires some risk.

2. Take risks only where you can handle the loss.

3. Adjust risks that are too much of a gamble.

4. Accept that the price of risking is occasional failure.

How would you characterize yourself when it comes to taking risks? Write your answer in the space below.

_____

_____

_____

_____

_____

RISK-MANAGEMENT GUIDELINES

- Review your motivation to become a consultant. Decide again why it is important to become a consultant. Ask yourself: Is the risk of failing to become a successful consultant worth the possible gain of succeeding?

- Recognize your risk-taking tendencies. Understand any bias you may have—either toward seeking risk or toward avoiding it.

- Develop your transition strategy for becoming self-employed.

- Increase your chances of success by gathering information that helps you make more informed, low-risk decisions.

(For more information on risk taking see author? *Risk Taking: A Guide for Decision Makers*, Crisp Publications. It will teach you how to manage risk more effectively.)

THE JUMP STARTER   *CASE STUDY NO. 5*

Ken had come into a large company as a technical staff member specializing in the analysis of engineering problems. As part of a midcareer renewal effort, he obtained a business degree to complement his engineering degree.

His role in the company didn't really allow him the opportunity to grow and take advantage of his considerable business acumen. Early on, he decided that some kind of consulting role would make better use of his talents.

Defining his niche of expertise, he networked actively in professional meetings and contacted numerous professional service and engineering businesses, advertising his availability as a consultant.

His break came when one of the engineering companies he had been in contact with approached him with an offer to start up a new business unit for them. It was in the area of his expertise, and he sold the company on the idea that he could handle the job better and cheaper as a consultant. He signed a one-year agreement to develop the new business area.

START-UP NEEDS

There are many needs for the start-up consultant. Many are highly recommended. Others can be considered optional, depending on your transitional situation. You must decide. Some require an investment in your practice. Others are cost-free. You need to decide how much you plan to invest in your new business.

Many people have gone through start-up on a shoe-string. Others have invested substantial sums. What is appropriate for you depends on many variables, including your commitment to becoming an independent consultant.

Many people ease into their own business with as little investment as possible. Others go full steam ahead because they are highly committed, or because they have the resources to do it. No doubt it's easier when you have all the tools, but that does not guarantee you will make it quickly, or even ultimately succeed.

Remember your image and reputation. Before you decide what you will require, think what your prospective clients expect from you. You are building a reputation and image, and many of the items you need will be a reflection of your image.

THE RETIREE

CASE STUDY NO. 6

Bob had worked for the government for 25 years as a geographer. During that time he earned the traditional promotions, and even got to take a year off to go to an Ivy League school for some "cutting edge" training in his specialty. As retirement time loomed, he realized he'd had enough of the day-to-day rigors (and boredom) of his job. When offered an early-out retirement, he jumped at the opportunity.

Within six months, he found himself bored and suffering from a serious case of "cabin fever." He missed some of the challenges of the workplace environment, but had no regrets about not being a full-time employee. Getting back in touch with his profession (by attending several professional conferences and exhibitions), he realized that his years of experience were still an asset to the planning, engineering, and environmental organizations that were attempting to apply cutting-edge technology.

If he could just package himself in the right way, he could get the professional stimulation he missed, earn a modest amount of money, and still have time to do some serious fishing several times a year.

His solution was to offer himself as a mentor or coaching consultant to companies with junior professional staff trying to apply new geographic-analysis technologies. By working essentially as an in-house consultant, he was able to recapture that sense of professional challenge he missed, make a reasonable consulting fee, and have the personal flexibility to enjoy his real passion—fishing.

INVESTMENTS IN YOUR PRACTICE

Here's a list of items you may need. In the first column, write *yes* or *no* to indicate if that item is required. In the second column, estimate the dollar amount for those items that require an initial one-time investment, such as business cards. In the third column, estimate any ongoing monthly expenses, such as telephone service.

	Required	Initial Outlay	Monthly Expense
Company name	_____	_____	_____
Company brochure	_____	_____	_____
Business cards	_____	_____	_____
Stationery and envelopes with logo	_____	_____	_____
Office space	_____	_____	_____
Office furniture	_____	_____	_____
Copying machine	_____	_____	_____
Fax machine	_____	_____	_____
Computer for word processing	_____	_____	_____
Software programs	_____	_____	_____
Licenses, permits, or registrations	_____	_____	_____
Automobile	_____	_____	_____
Bank account	_____	_____	_____
Supplies	_____	_____	_____
Specialized equipment	_____	_____	_____
Telephone service	_____	_____	_____

	Required	Initial Outlay	Monthly Expense
Answering machine or service	_____	_____	_____
Business insurance	_____	_____	_____
Bookkeeping or accounting system	_____	_____	_____
Line of credit	_____	_____	_____
Form of business (sole proprietorship, partnership, or corporation)	_____	_____	_____
Advice from an attorney	_____	_____	_____
Advice from an accountant	_____	_____	_____
Advice from a marketing consultant	_____	_____	_____
Creation of a business plan	_____	_____	_____
Additional wardrobe	_____	_____	_____
Others: _____	_____	_____	_____
Total number of items required (add up those checked *yes*)	_____		
Total initial investment (add up column 2)		$ _____	
Ongoing monthly expenses (add up column 3)			$ _____

Now you can see what it will probably cost you to go into business, and you can estimate your monthly overhead. Compared to the $250,000 it costs to open a small restaurant in a metropolitan area, getting into consulting is rather inexpensive and entails a minimum financial risk.

Your return on investment needs to be examined. That is, what do you think you will make on your investment? Any money you invest in your business should bring a return. With that in mind, investing in your business should not be so difficult, but something you want to do!

START-UP FINANCIAL RESOURCES

The day you make your initial investment in your practice will be one you remember. Until then, it is useful to determine just where the financial resources for start-up will come from.

Re-examine the total initial investment required to start your practice: $_____. (See the total from "Investments In Your Practice.")

Where do you intend to get the financial resources you need to start-up your consulting practice?

Check ☑ all those resources that you plan to use. Estimate percentages from each source.

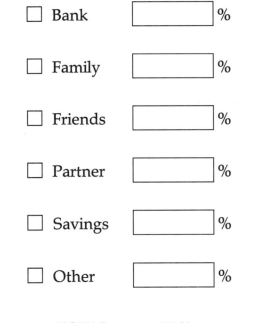

☐ Bank		%
☐ Family		%
☐ Friends		%
☐ Partner		%
☐ Savings		%
☐ Other		%

TOTAL   100%

If you are unsure where your resources will come from, it may be time to re-examine what it will take to launch your consulting practice. Remember, being undercapitalized is the main reason given for business failures. Having sufficient financial resources to successfully launch a consulting practice is critical for your success.

THE LATE BLOOMER

CASE STUDY NO. 7

Jim had always been a searcher. In the 60s, he searched for the meaning of life and truth. In the 70s, he searched for professional identity. In the 80s, he continued this search for his professional identity. This constant search included forays into graduate degree programs, professional development workshops, and considerable involvement in the activities of various professional associations. The bottom line was that Jim had not yet found his real sense of professional identity.

At family get-togethers, friends' parties, and even class reunions, it was apparent that Jim had always taken the alternative route when it came to professional identity. Aware of this, but not overly concerned, he continued on his open-ended search, going from job to job, never really being either challenged or satisfied.

Finally, he was faced with several difficult life events that brought the futility of this searching into perspective. Allowing a little attention to be focused on what he did best, as opposed to the wide range of his capabilities, which all had potential, he focused on specific consulting skills and specific knowledge areas where he knew he had talent. What remained was to muster the motivation to be competitive.

This is where the energy and discipline learned in his searching efforts paid off. As a late-blooming consultant, he now enjoys the recognition and identity which he longed for, and with it has come the satisfaction of seeing the value of his efforts.

TRANSITION PLAN

Detail below just how you plan to make your transition. Be as detailed as possible. (Be sure to read all the case studies first.)

I plan to _____

_____

_____

My initial source(s) of clients will be _____

_____

_____

My initial source(s) of income will be _____

_____

_____

I characterize myself as (entrepreneur, part-timer, etc.—see the Case Studies)

_____

_____

I plan to leave full-time employment on (date): _____

_____

I plan to be fully functioning as an independent consultant on _____

_____

YOUR CASE STUDY

Now you're ready to write your own case study in the space below. Write three or four short paragraphs, based on the exercises you've done in this part.

_____

_____

_____

_____

_____

_____

_____

_____

_____

_____

_____

_____

_____

_____

_____

_____

_____

_____

_____

_____

_____

P A R T

5

Marketing Consulting Services

WHY CONSULTANTS ARE HIRED

It is important to understand why consultants are hired, since it will shape the approach you take in selling your services. The approach taken here is termed *consultive client-driven selling*, because identifying the prospective client's needs is foremost.

As you might suspect, there is no single reason consultants are hired. What follows is a list of the many possible reasons. Which reasons apply to hiring you, given the consultancy you are thinking of creating? How will the reasons affect your selling style? Put a check ☑ next to each one that may apply to your consulting practice.

☐ 1. *The skills needed are not available within the organization.*   Outside help is the only way to get the skills needed to solve the problem or complete the project.

☐ 2. *In-house people don't have time.*   Even if the organization has the expertise for the project, house staff cannot take time away from their regular work.

☐ 3. *Organizations want a fresh perspective on their problem or business.*   Organizations want the new ideas only an outsider can provide, or they want an independent, unbiased point of view.

☐ 4. *Prospects cannot identify what needs to be done.*   Consultants can provide an objective assessment of a situation and help define the problem.

☐ 5. *A consultant may be faster and more cost-effective than in-house staff.*   Consultants who have worked on a particular project many times can often do it faster and more skillfully than in-house staff, and sometimes at a lower cost.

☐ 6. *Consultants are hired to provide a second opinion.*   In-house approaches often miss the mark because the staff is too close to the problem.

☐ 7. *Consultants allow flexibility in staffing.*   When the project ends, the organization can end the consulting relationship easily and quickly. With a consultant, there is no long-term obligation, or concern about wrongful-discharge suits.

WHY CONSULTANTS ARE HIRED (Continued)

☐ **8.** *Consultants are hired on a temporary basis.* Often, the organization does not want to hire a permanent professional staffer for reasons such as limited funding or a possible financial downturn.

☐ **9.** *Consultants are hired in crisis situations.* A problem has gotten out of hand and needs immediate attention. Consultants can attack a problem and provide immediate results. Hiring and training new staff is time-consuming.

☐ **10.** *Consultants are hired to deal with complex organizational problems.* Often, only an outsider can see duplication of effort and ill-conceived organizational structures that impair growth and responsiveness to the organization's customers.

☐ **11.** *Consultants are often hired to aid executives who perceive their own weaknesses.* They know that outside help can aid in identifying problems and potential solutions, as well as in implementing them.

☐ **12.** Others: _____

You should determine the specific reason(s) you would be hired in any given situation, and *sell yourself* accordingly!

(For more insights, especially from the organization's perspective, see *Selecting and Working with Consultants*, Crisp Publications.

MARKETING SKILLS

Marketing skills are necessary if one is to be successful in launching and maintaining a thriving consultancy. The most frequent reason for a failed consultancy is the lack of a cohesive marketing program. (See David Karlson, *Marketing Your Consulting or Professional Services*, Crisp Publications, for more detailed information on marketing.)

The consultant-skills audit that you completed in Part 2 asked you to rate your skills in this important area. In this part of the book we will examine more closely what marketing a start-up consulting practice involves.

MISSION STATEMENT

A mission statement defines your consultancy. It enables you to clarify your purpose to anyone you engage—from your banker to prospective clients. Further, it differentiates you from the crowded field so that you stand out.

Consider the following examples of mission statements for various consulting firms.

- Computer consulting firm:
  Provide computer consulting services to small and midsized companies in all aspects of accounting systems.

- Management consulting firm:
  Provide management consulting in the area of organizational development to facilitate reorganization in large corporations.

- Personnel consulting firm:
  Design training programs that respond to the unique training needs of middle managers.

- Information systems consulting firm:
  Design and install management information systems for midsized retail sales organizations.

- Marketing consulting firm:
  Assist small and midsized firms by providing marketing advice and developing comprehensive marketing programs.

DEVELOP YOUR MISSION STATEMENT

Now see if you can write your own mission statement. In the space below, write the type of consulting firm you intend to start, and your mission statement.

- _____
  _____
  _____

DESCRIPTION OF THE SERVICE

The mission statement gives the big picture of your business. Now you want to specify in greater detail the services you plan to offer. For example, in the case of a marketing consulting firm, a more detailed description of services would be:

1. Marketing planning

2. Service positioning

3. Creation of promotional strategy

4. Selection of marketing tactics

5. Creation of marketing communications

6. Market research and evaluation

7. Program implementation

Try and see if you can list a more detailed description of the services you plan to provide. If you have trouble sharply defining the services you plan to offer, you need to ask yourself:

- Am I trying to do too much?

- By limiting my services, will I gain a focus upon which to build my reputation?

- By defining my services very specifically, will I look more like the expert that prospects want to hire?

- By specializing, will it be easier to communicate what I do for prospective clients?

- By being _too_ specialized, will I have too few clients to support a consulting practice?

SPECIFIC SERVICES YOU PLAN TO OFFER

1. _____
2. _____
3. _____
4. _____
5. _____
6. _____

WHO ARE YOUR POTENTIAL CLIENTS?

Now that you are able to articulate your services, who will use your services? List them here.

The types of clients I would like to serve are:

1. _____
2. _____
3. _____
4. _____
5. _____
6. _____

If you are having trouble, you may need to do more research on who might use your services. Or it might be that you don't know how to segment your market (i.e., what part of the market you want to serve). As you consider your prospective clientele, think in terms of demographics, such as age, sex, or income.

For example, your client might be government. But within government, you might want to serve federal instead of state, county, or local municipalities. In addition, you might want to serve federal agencies whose main function is service.

Or you might discriminate by size of business (small, medium, large); by particular types of consumers (elderly, youth, yuppy, single parents); or by types of businesses (manufacturing, high-tech, retailing, nonprofit, trade associations).

MARKET RESEARCH

After you decide what services you will offer to prospective clients, it is important to determine:

- Do they really want it?

- Is it the right service for them?

- If not, what do they really want or need?

- Can you demonstrate the demand for the service?

You can do your market research by phone, in person, or in informal groups.

Using the phone involves simply calling prospects and asking:

1. What problems are you having in relation to the services I will be offering?

2. How do you go about currently solving the problem?

Personal meetings with prospects follow the same approach, except that appointments are usually made. One thing is for sure, by talking with prospective clients you will gather much valuable information that will sharpen your market focus. And these calls will save a lot of time and energy you might spend needlessly should you offer services without determining the demand for them.

An informal market research group involves bringing prospective users together (five to ten) and getting their reaction to the services you plan to offer. They are asked to react on the basis of their needs and experience. Again, you will gain a lot of valuable information that will help you sharpen your focus.

A final word on market research: Before deciding consulting is for you, doing the market research will tell you much about the type of people you would be serving, the expectations they have of consultants, and whether you would like to work for them. Doing your market research *now* will help to answer the question: "Is consulting for me?" You can't afford to skip this important step.

KNOW YOUR COMPETITION

As a professional, your clients expect you to know your competition. If you don't, it could prove embarrassing and breed a lack of confidence in your business skills. Find out who is in the consulting service area you are exploring. Frequently, other professionals are happy to talk with a newcomer, because although today you are a competitor, tomorrow you might be a collaborator on a large joint venture.

As you talk to others who are actively engaged in the consulting field you intend to enter, find out:

1. What is the nature of competition in the field? Is it highly competitive and crowded with consultants? If so, what are the implications for your practice? Will you face little or no competition because of the uniqueness of your services?

2. Is the field in which you plan to consult relatively new? If so, does your competition have to educate prospects about the use of consultants before prospects will contract for services?

3. Is your consulting field undergoing major change? Is the change caused by internal forces or influenced by forces outside the field (for example, the state of the economy)?

4. What specific services does the competition provide?

5. What does your competition promote the hardest?

6. How do your competitors promote their consulting services?

7. The status of the local field: Who is retiring? Who has lost what accounts? What new projects are forthcoming?

Armed with good information, you will be in a better position to decide how to go about promoting your services. In addition, you will have a much better idea of how the field functions, and whether it is for you.

PROMOTING YOUR SERVICES

Promotion means getting prospective clients to inquire about your services or creating any opportunity that allows you to sell your services to inquirers. When you are clear about the consulting services you offer and the prospective clients you would like to reach, promotion becomes a matter of choosing your strategy.

A *fast-growth strategy* usually involves more expensive promotional techniques. A *slow-growth strategy* is personally time-consuming as well as labor intensive, and it takes longer to build a client base. You will need to decide which is best for you based on your budget, your personal likes and dislikes, and your ability to employ the promotional techniques you are considering.

The more promotion you do, the faster your practice grows. Some promotional techniques require time and energy and tend to be inexpensive. Others are expensive yet reach more prospects and result in more inquiries. Also, you must consider if you are capable of using a particular promotional technique. Additional exploration is required on promotional techniques to determine the skill level required. To help this exploration, each of the sections that follow lists useful sources of information.

Following are the most popular promotional techniques used by consultants, with a brief explanation of each. You decide which ones you might use in building your consulting practice, which ones you can afford, and which ones you need to explore further.

SEMINARS AND WORKSHOPS

Seminars and workshops are a very popular means to introduce potential clients to pertinent information, such as information on new tax laws. They are short in duration, usually lasting no more than a week and commonly a day or less. They are educational, providing either information alone or information plus hands-on training and skill building. Tuition fees can vary from no charge to hundreds of dollars per day. Seminars and workshops may be used as a PR tool to attract new clients, or they may be used solely to generate profits for the practice.

Tuition-free seminars and workshops are frequently used to introduce potential clients to cutting-edge knowledge in a very condensed format. The objective may be to introduce your service to prospective new clients. This can be an expensive marketing tactic, however, because it is generally promoted by a combination of direct mail, paid advertisements, and telemarketing.

For more information on seminars and workshops:

1. See Herman Holtz, *Expanding Your Consulting Practice with Seminars*, Wiley, 1987.
2. See reference books on direct mail (e.g., E. L. Nash, *Direct Marketing*, McGraw-Hill, 1986). Seminars are promoted frequently by direct-mail brochures.
3. Attend a seminar in your field and talk to the sponsor to determine what was involved.
4. See L. Munson, *How to Conduct Training Seminars*, McGraw-Hill, 1987.

TELEMARKETING

Potential clients are contacted by telephone to generate interest in your services. The goal is to gain the opportunity to meet prospects personally and discuss how you could assist them. There is usually no obligation or cost to the potential client for an initial meeting. At the meeting you collect information about the potential client's needs so that you will be able to respond more fully on how you can serve them.

For more information on telemarketing:

1. Contact your local phone company for training on telemarketing, which could be valuable.

2. See L. Finch, *Telephone Courtesy and Customer Service*, Crisp Publications, and D. Scott, *Time Management and the Telephone*, Crisp Publications, for basics on telephone usage.

3. See J. Freestone and J. Brusse, *Telemarketing Basics*, Crisp Publications, for the basics.

4. See M. Roman, *Telemarketing Campaigns That Work*, 1986, and *Telephone Marketing*, McGraw-Hill, 1987.

5. See R. McHatton, *Total Telemarketing*, Wiley, 1987.

DIRECT MAIL

Direct mail is a fast-growing marketing tactic, because its results are predictable. Direct mail involves mailing hundreds of thousands of brochures, letters, or a combination of a letters and brochures to potential clients. Highly specialized mailing lists are used, so that the direct-mail piece is placed directly into the hands of the potential client.

Direct mail is often used in combination with telemarketing. The direct-mail piece might describe the needs of the client and how your service can satisfy those needs. After the impersonal direct-mail piece is sent out, a personal telephone follow-up is made, to emphasize the value of your service to the potential client. An attempt can be made to meet with the potential client to further discuss his or her needs or to fulfill an offer you have made, such as participation in a free seminar.

For more information on direct mail:

1. Contact the local chapter of the Direct Marketing Association, which offers listings of firms that specialize in direct mail and telemarketing.

2. Attend a seminar on the topic, such as those conducted by the Direct Marketing Association, 6 East 43rd St., New York, NY 10017.

3. See Edward Nash, *Direct Marketing*, McGraw-Hill, 1986.

4. See Jim Kobs, *Profitable Direct Marketing*, Crain Books, 1989.

5. See Rose Harper, *Mailing List Strategies, McGraw-Hill, 1989.*

6. See Charles Mallory's *Direct Mail Magic*, Crisp Publications, 1991, in the back of this book.

PROMOTING YOUR SERVICES (Continued)

LECTURES AND SPEECHES

Organizations frequently seek interesting, educational, motivational, entertaining, thought-provoking speakers to address their members. You can use speeches as a mechanism to educate audiences about your field and to promote your practice indirectly. You appear as an expert sharing what you know about your field and doing so in the interest of your audience. Hence you gain credibility.

Speeches are usually a half-hour to an hour long. They can be on topics directly associated with your profession. Topics may also be unrelated to your profession but about an interest you have outside of your profession, such as sailing or bird watching.

You can register with speakers' bureaus, professional organizations, the Chamber of Commerce, and college and universities that recommend speakers as a part of their efforts to provide public services to the community. You can directly contact organizations whose members fit the description of the new clients you would like to reach. Many of these organizations have regular meetings (for example, Kiwanis or Rotary) and are anxious to have their members learn about new approaches to commonly shared problems.

For more information on giving speeches:

1. Contact your local Toastmasters organization if you want the opportunity to hone your speechmaking skills before going public with this tactic.

2. Check with educational institutions in your area for courses and programs on verbal communication.

3. Order S. Mandel, *Effective Presentation Skills*, for the basics on presentations using the back of this book.

4. Contact organizations like the Chamber of Commerce, Rotary, or Jaycees, to determine what topics are of interest to their members.

5. Call your local chapter of the National Speakers Association, which offers many opportunities for members to improve their speaking techniques.

6. See Margaret Bedrosian, *Speak Like a Pro*, Wiley, 1987, for a very insightful approach to speechmaking.

7. See B. Decker, *The Art of Communicating*, Crisp Publications, for powerful communications techniques using the back of this book.

NETWORKING WITH THE COMPETITION

Nearly every field has a professional association through which you can inform other professionals about your practice. Professional associations provide numerous member services, including educational programs that keep you current on advances in the field, and specialty subgroups for members with similar interests. Regular meetings and publications are usually offered. The opportunity to interact with others in the field is invaluable. A competitor one day may be a collaborator the next.

Business organizations such as the Chamber of Commerce give you the opportunity to meet various professionals who may become clients or may be able to make referrals to you. Business organizations can also represent the collective interests of the business community to government agencies and the general community, including schools, planning agencies, and so on.

The Small Business Administration (SBA) sponsors programs to aid business development that might contribute to building your practice. SBA sponsors and funds programs at colleges and universities with the sole purpose of aiding businesses in all aspects, including marketing. These organizations publish and distribute directories of businesses and professionals serving the community. County and state agencies of economic development also have programs to attract and assist small business.

Networking also involves letting anyone know who might help build your practice, including associates from all your previous employers, college friends, and avocational contacts. Announce your new firm to them, and ask them if they know anyone who can use your services.

For more information on professional organizations and networking:

1. Contact the membership director of your local Chamber of Commerce.

2. Call your local colleges or universities that conduct SBA-sponsored programs.

3. Contact state, municipal, and county offices of economic development for a calendar of events.

4. Contact the local chapter of your primary professional organization and those of allied fields.

5. See the *Encyclopedia of Associations*, Gale Research, published annually. It lists professional consulting associations from all fields.

6. See Robert Elster, editor, *Small Business Sourcebook*, Gale Research, 1987.

7. See V. Johnson, *Effective Networking*, Crisp Publications, 1990, using the back of this book.

8. Make a list of all the individuals who could be part of your extended network.

PROMOTING YOUR SERVICES (Continued)

REFERRALS

A personal referral occurs when a client, associate, or competitor recommends your services to a potential client. Referrals from clients, associates, and others are an excellent source for gaining new clients. Referrals can be secured by: (1) requesting and encouraging referrals, verbally or in writing, from current clients; (2) participating in a referral network with other professionals; and (3) soliciting referrals from other professionals who might be too busy to handle the type of clients you are interested in serving.

In order to reward referrals, consider offering a fee for any referral that turns into a paying client. The fee might range from a token to a significant percentage of your fee, depending on the nature of your profession. Referral fees are easily justified since referrals save you the time and the expense associated with attracting new clients. If fees are not considered appropriate in your field, you may want to offer in-kind services or barter in some fashion to encourage referrals.

Once a referral is made, it is extremely important to follow up with both the potential client and the party who made the referral. Acknowledging your appreciation for referrals is essential if you expect continued referrals.

For more information on referrals and referral fees:
1. Consult with your professional organization to determine the current practices in your field.
2. Talk with others in your field to see what their policies are for referral fees.
3. See Robert Elster, editor, *Small Business Sourcebook*, Gale Research, 1987.

CONFERENCE PRESENTATIONS AND TRADE-SHOW EXHIBITS

Conferences, conventions, and trade shows are usually sponsored by organizations such as community colleges, county offices of economic development, chambers of commerce, professional associations, and libraries. They provide an opportunity for you to reach a large number of people in a concentrated period of time. The risk and expense of promoting the event are the responsibility of the sponsor.

If you make a presentation, it is usually to a large number of potential clients. You must make a presentation that relates to the theme of the event as well as to your practice.

If you rent an exhibit booth or have a display, you usually are charged for the space. However, you will have the opportunity to meet large numbers of potential clients on a personal basis.

For more information on conference presentations and trade-show exhibits:

1. Determine the types of conventions your prospective clients attend and where you could make presentations.
2. Contact a local chapter of the Exhibit Designers and Producers Association for professional assistance in creating an exhibit or display.
3. See E. A. Chapman, *Exhibit Making*, McGraw-Hill, 1987.

SOCIAL, RELIGIOUS AND OTHER ORGANIZATIONS

There are numerous organizations unrelated to your field that can be advantageous to join. People are notoriously curious about how others make their living, and no doubt you will have the opportunity to discuss your practice and gain referrals.

Also, as society becomes more complex, membership in organizations becomes a way of meeting people with similar values and interests. The underlying assumption with this tactic is that potential clients like to do business with people they know and trust. By being active in a variety of organizations, you have the opportunity to associate with more people and increase your exposure, while doing something you enjoy.

For more information on social and other organizations:
1. Service organizations: Contact such organizations as Rotary, Kiwanis, Lions, Red Cross, Cancer Society, and the Kidney Foundation.
2. Social: Contact your alumni associations and special-interest clubs, such as the local bridge club, garden society, and square dancing club.
3. Civic: Contact county-wide and local civic organizations. Your local municipality maintains listings.
4. Religious: Within religious groups there are often business support groups.

TEACHING

Numerous organizations offer courses whose subject matter may be directly related to your service. For example, ''Financial Planning for Retirement,'' ''Computerizing Your Small Business Accounting System,'' ''Stepping Up to Supervisor,'' are typical courses offered for credit and noncredit by colleges, universities, community college, libraries, professional associations, the YMCA, and other educational organizations.

Instructors are selected on the basis of their educational credentials and, more often, for their work-related experience. Courses range in length from a half-day to a semester. As an instructor, you are usually paid a modest stipend and your name is listed in class schedules that are widely distributed in the community. Obviously, you can make personal contact with potential clients who attend.

For more information on teaching opportunities:
1. Contact your local educational institutions (colleges, board of educations, etc.) to determine instructor requirements. In addition, ask what courses they would like to see created in your field, since they are interested in providing innovative courses or seminars.
2. Check with your local reference librarian to determine what types of nontraditional institutions also offer educational programs. For example, the Chamber of Commerce offers courses to assist members in conducting their businesses.
3. Call your local Small Business Administration office for course information.

PROMOTING YOUR SERVICES (Continued)

WRITING AND PUBLISHING A NEWSLETTER

Newsletters are usually from one to four pages long. They contain short articles that focus on particular needs or interests of the readers. Some newsletters are cost-free to the reader, and merely present information that educates the client about your field or practice without directly promoting your service. Newsletters are very popular in all segments of the professional business world.

In contrast, subscription newsletters are themselves income-producing and contain critical information necessary to conduct business. The subscription fee can range from a modest amount to several hundred dollars yearly. An example of revenue-producing newsletters might provide the latest information on federal legislation and its impact on the oil industry.

Newsletters can be published on both regular and irregular schedules, depending on their purpose. They use mailing lists that can include hundreds or thousands of names.

For more information on newsletters:
1. Find out from your professional organization what generic newsletters are available.
2. Contact printers for cost estimates, and ask your postmaster about a bulk mail permit.
3. Contact the Newsletter Association, 1401 Wilson Blvd., Arlington, VA 22009, for information on their newsletter seminars.

WRITING FOR PUBLICATION

You can write feature articles for magazines and journals, author a book or monograph, write book reviews, and submit letters to the editor. All these tactics can be used to communicate important educational information or knowledge about your field. Once published, written information can be used repeatedly and shared widely.

Organizations with publications are frequently looking for feature articles that are relevant to their readers. You can redirect the focus of an article you have written to convey your message to a new readership. Thus you can gain exposure to a new potential client market. For example, an article on ''Financial Planning for the Elderly'' could be refocused to become an article on ''Financial Planning for Those with Elderly Parents.''

Associations publish journals, for which you can write articles. You might consider reprinting articles you write for distribution to prospects, along with a promotional letter.

Writing a book or monograph is a major undertaking, but it is sometimes worth the effort because it contributes to your reputation. Publishers are usually willing to listen to ideas you have for a book, and they may suggest topics of interest in your field.

Book reviews enable you to demonstrate your breadth of knowledge. They are sought out by professional organizations for inclusion in their newsletters or journals.

A letter to the editor allows you to comment on materials the newspaper or journal has published. Without great effort, you can give your view and gain exposure to the readership.

For more information on writing for publication:

1. Contact the publications editors of organizations whose publications are read by your potential clients, to see what topics in your field would be relevant and what ones they would accept.

2. Contact professionals for help with your writing. Any piece going into publication is best served by the review of a professional writer or editor.

3. Review trade and professional journals for ideas on subject matter of interest to readers in your field.

4. Check your library reference section for books on all aspects of publishing, for example: S. Burack, editor, *The Writer's Handbook,* Writers Inc., 1987; R. Balkin, *A Writer's Guide to Book Publishing*, Hawthorn/Dutton, 1981.

DIRECTORIES AND DATABASES

Numerous directories are published listing professional service providers. The most common one is the Yellow Pages. Professional organizations usually publish directories as a method of promoting the professions. Some listings are expensive, depending on the size and nature of your listing. Others are free.

With the advent of the personal computer, databases that contain information on almost every subject, including listings of service providers, are readily available. Your practice is probably eligible to be listed on a database and you don't even know it! Database usage is growing rapidly in this age of information.

When you review a directory, be sure to determine all the ways you could be listed; for example, as a consultant, management consultant, and so on. Think of all the ways in which prospective clients might perceive your profession and might approach your service in a directory.

As more individuals provide services of all types, specialized directories have become more popular. Access to up-to-date specialized information via computer has become more readily available and more commonly used.

PROMOTING YOUR SERVICES (Continued)

DIRECTORIES AND DATABASES (Continued)

For more information on directory listings and databases:
1. Contact your local Yellow Pages representative for details on being listed. Ask what has been effective for others who have listed. For example, using color in a listing gains more inquiries.
2. Check with your professional organization, community agencies, Chamber of Commerce, Small Business Administration, and Office of Economic Development about their directories and about other directories they can recommend in your field.
3. Ask your local reference librarian for the names of databases related to your type of business. Professional directories are a part of many business-related databases, such as DIALOG, LEXIS, NEXIS, PREDICASTS, and HRIN.
4. See Gale Research Company's *Consultants and Consulting Organizations Directory*. This database references information on more than 12,000 consultants and consulting organizations in 135 fields.

CAPABILITY BROCHURE

A capability brochure is much like a résumé, but instead of representing an individual it represents a business firm. A capability brochure conveys the firm's ability to deal with intangible problems and produce results. The format varies, depending on your profession and what you choose to include.

If you decide to create a capability brochure, you can distribute it with letters to potential clients as an introduction; give a supply to your prime accounts to pass on to interested colleagues; keep a few in your briefcase to leave with your card if you do personal selling; or use it in a direct mail solicitation.

Often you do not need a capability brochure because you are present to personally convey your capabilities. But in some situations you will need to make a presentation of your capabilities to a prospective client by mail.

A well-designed brochure gives your potential client an impression of you as a professional; an idea of what you can deliver; a sample of your background and experience; an impression of what it would be like to work with you; and a means to communicate your skills to others, including higher-level decision makers. A good capability brochure communicates the image that you want to project.

For more information on capability brochures:
1. If you don't have the skills to produce it yourself, contact a professional writer or marketing consultant for help.
2. Check with a printer for estimates on printing.
3. Ask a professional writer and a marketing consultant to evaluate a draft copy of your capability brochure. Initially print it using your personal computer and stationery, if you have a laser computer printer. This gives you an opportunity to get reactions before having it professionally printed.

MEDIA PUBLICITY

Conducting your own public-relations campaign can be worth thousands of dollars in advertising for your practice. The publicity you seek may concern anything relevant to your practice including announcements about new staff, obtaining new business contracts or clients, the release of information about new laws, a major accomplishment in your field, a unique approach to solving a particular problem, or innovative services you plan to offer. The information is usually made available to the media in a press release which you prepare.

The key to attracting media attention about any topic is simple—there must be a story that will be of interest to the audience. It is the media's job to cover stories and present news of general interest to their viewers or readers. To qualify, your *publicity* must be for an identifiable segment of the *public*. As you consider the various media available to you, determine to whom they appeal and the niche they hold in their respective markets. To retain a market, media have identified viewers or readers that are financially supportive. You must determine what media your prospective clients support, so that your publicity efforts can be targeted for the best results—producing favorable publicity for your practice.

The number of media through which you try to gain publicity will vary depending on your potential clientele. Media for a general audience includes print (newspapers and magazines of all types) and radio or TV (news, talk shows, features shows). Media for a specialized audience might include those that cover only business and finance, men or women, military, travel, associations, clubs, fraternal organizations, trades (technical), ethnic groups, religion, retirees, or sports.

The form you use for the publicity will vary, but could include a press release, an appearance on a radio or TV talk show, an interview with a newscaster, a feature story in a newspaper or magazine, a quotation of your opinion as an expert about an event in your field, or a reference to your activities in the calendar section of a newspaper or journal.

For more information on media publicity:

1. See F. Danzing and T. Klein, *Publicity: How to Make Media Work for You*, Scribner, 1985.

2. See L. Gordon, *How to Handle Your Own Public Relations*, Nelson Hall, 1976.

3. See *Publicity Power*, Crisp Publications, 1988.

THE ROLE OF PERSONAL SELLING

Let's begin with a test to examine your perceptions about the role of selling in consulting. Be candid and answer with your innermost feelings about selling.

Circle T for *true* or F for *false*.

T F Selling has a significant role in consulting.

T F Selling has a bad image among those considering consulting, because its role is frequently misunderstood.

T F Selling can be rewarding, especially if the consultant is better able to determine the prospect's needs.

T F The selling of intangible services must be fully understood to appreciate the role of selling in consulting.

T F Successful consultants are good at selling their services because they understand clients' buying behaviors.

T F Successful consultants enjoy selling their services.

T F Effective selling is client driven, not seller driven.

T F Prospective clients demand the opportuntity to be sold to by consultants.

T F No matter how much a consulting practice is promoted, someone in the firm will have to meet with the prospect to close the sale.

T F Selling consulting services takes several skills, including the ability to listen carefully, to interpret needs, to identify problems, to provide potential solutions, and to ask probing questions.

T F Consultive selling affords you the opportunity to gain the confidence of the prospect early, since the prospect senses early in the call that you are looking out for his or her best interests, not just your own.

How did you do?

If you circled T for every one, you got a perfect score and are well on your way to understanding the role of selling in consulting. If you circled any Fs, read on and see if you don't change your mind about the role of selling.

Yes, consulting involves selling! Let's examine why and how your perception of professional service selling might change if it happens to be negative. Once your practice has been promoted (by whatever means you selected from the long list of promotional tactics), you begin to get your first inquiries or referrals from prospects. How you respond is critical to getting clients. Remember nothing happens unless there is a *sale*.

PERSONAL SELLING

Personal selling plays a major role in acquiring new clients. Regardless of what marketing tactics you employ, personal selling is usually required at some point to secure clients. To some extent, all employees of a professional service firm play a role in selling—from those that answer the phone to those that meet with prospects to finalize the contract for services.

There is a unique feature to the selling and buying process associated with providing intangible services: potential clients generally want—and often demand—that the professional who sells the service must also perform the service. By necessity then, professionals must take on a sales role if they are to satisfy the needs of their prospects. Prospects want personal interaction *before* they become clients. This uniqueness in the selling and buying process is caused by the highly personal nature of professional services. The client often directly participates with the professional in some role, either passively or actively.

Not surprisingly then, prospective clients want the opportunity to personally interact with the professional. They want to assess numerous factors which they consider important in their selection of a consultant. Let the client's needs be foremost in your efforts to sell your services.

Finally, the legal and ethical rules of your profession may govern the extent of your personal selling efforts. The use of marketing tactics that are less personal for gaining inquiries from prospective clients (e.g., brochures, directory listings) may be dictated by the acceptable standards of your profession.

The power of personal consultive selling:

1. It gives you the opportunity to meet the prospect face to face, enabling you to establish a personal working relationship.

2. Professional services are often contracted for based on the personal experience the potential client (the buyer) has with the professional (the seller).

3. Personal selling allows for direct communication between the seller and buyer, which allows you to make your best case based on sound information, including the opportunity to determine if you want to serve a particular client.

4. Personal selling, although labor-intensive and costly, is an effective method to gain clients and can give you valuable information on the needs of clients, which you can translate into new services.

PERSONAL SELLING (Continued)

The pitfalls of personal selling:

1. Consultants are sometimes uncomfortable selling, since it has not been traditional for professionals to have to sell their devices.

2. If seen merely as a necessary evil, selling can have a negative impact on your firm.

3. If personal selling skills are not sharpened and honed for the competitive arena, professionals can damage their reputation.

4. Selling is time-consuming and can be exhausting. It may require repeated interaction before a prospect becomes a paying client.

For more information on personal selling:

1. See R. Morgan, *Professional Sales Training*, Crisp Publications, 1988.

2. See W. Bolen, *Creative Selling: The Competitive Edge*, U.S. Small Business Administration, 1985.

P A R T

6

Dealing with Clients

THE FIRST MEETING

Interpersonal skills are the engine for your sales behavior in first meetings, as you determine if this is a prospect for whom you would like to work. These skills should complement your selling skills.

How well do you relate? Circle *yes* or *no* below.

Your social skills are important as you try to relate to strangers! Are you good at:

Yes No   1. *Small talk:* The ability to put the client at ease before starting more serious discussions. (See L. Waymon and A. Baber, *Great Connections: Small Talk and Networking for Business People*, Impact, for terrific ways to enhance your gift of the gab.)

Yes No   2. *Listening:* The ability to listen and absorb critical information. (See D. Bone, *The Business of Listening*, Crisp Publications, for methods to improve your listening capabilities.

Yes No   3. *Making positive first impressions:* Remember you only get to make a first impression once! If you are comfortable with yourself and have clearly defined your consulting practice, you should be ready.

Yes No   4. *Thinking on your feet:* You will be expected to present yourself not only to individuals but also to groups. Good verbal communication skills are expected.

Yes No   5. *Projecting a professional image:* A firm handshake and a good overall appearance are what make for favorable impressions. Consider the image you will project. See D. Pooser, *Always in Style,* Crisp Publications for tips on dress, etc.

Yes No   6. *Presenting a positive personality:* Remember your wit, humor, charm, and intellectual curiosity. Use all your capabilities.

Yes, it takes a lot of interpersonal skills to be a consultant. Get friends and associates to assess your interpersonal skills, too. Sometimes we need candid feedback from outside to assess just how we really come across.

SHARPENING YOUR CONSULTIVE SELLING SKILLS

If you are client-oriented, your consultive selling skills are focused on:

1. Determining the reasons that a consultant is being hired.

   • Has the prospect had experience with consultants?

   • If so, what was that experience like?

   • Carefully review the reasons as outlined in Part 5.

2. Discussing the problems or issues faced by the client with as much detail as possible.

3. Discussing the prospective client's expectations of the consultancy.

4. Discussing various ways the problem might be approached—your behavior is consultive from the very beginning of the relationship.

5. Reading the prospect to assess how much solution information you will have to volunteer to gain his or her confidence. You have to give something away to demonstrate your capability. But put a limit on it, otherwise you'll look amateurish.

6. Recognizing what type of consulting work the prospect has in mind.

Remember, using the consultive approach to selling allows you to build confidence and trust with your prospect. They intuitively sense that you are acting in *their* best interest, not your own! Prospects are experts in contracting for services.

TAKING NOTES

Taking notes shows that you take the prospective client seriously. Don't rely on your memory. There is a lot to absorb as you make your first impression with your prospect. Put your energy into listening. Taking brief notes forces you to listen.

The first meeting involves a great deal of give and take between you and the prospect. A lot of sharing. A lot of relationship building—building a relationship may be at the top of the agenda for the first meeting. The key question underlying behavior is, "Can I work with this consultant?" And vice versa.

Ending the meeting

All good things must end! It is important to end the meeting with a clear understanding of the next step and of what is expected of the consultant.

Most frequently, a prospect will ask the consultant to submit a proposal. Proposals vary in scope and purpose, but they clearly require written communication skills.

The results you can expect

If you use your consultive selling skills at each meeting, you can expect:

- Much better prospect meetings

- A better understanding of each prospect's objectives or problems

- Many ideas for new services you might offer

- A more trusting relationship with each prospect

- Promotions that are client-driven

- An ability to do better consulting

- More productive sales calls

- More referrals from clients

DETERMINING THE SCOPE OF THE WORK

After the initial meeting, various methods can be used to determine the scope of the consulting work, and how much it will cost. Consultants contract to do work; there are many methods of contracting—from a handshake to a formal legal contract.

All of the methods—preproposals, formal proposals, contracts, and letters of agreement—require a sense of organization and written communication skills. The one that is right for you may be dictated by prospects or by your profession. As you read on, assess your writing skills.

PREPROPOSALS

Prospective clients often ask for a proposal that addresses their specific needs. Fully developed proposals take time to prepare and often require more information than you have at this stage. In addition, you have no assurance that you will be compensated for your efforts should you develop a full proposal.

One method to gain the client's confidence and satisfy a proposal request is to provide a prelimary proposal, or preproposal, which will serve as an entree to further discussion with the client. You might also use this approach as a technique to gain inquiries—by offering a no-cost, no-obligation preproposal to prospective clients. Be sure to advise the potential client of the limitations of your preproposal; that it represents your best thinking on the situation after just one meeting.

A preproposal, also known as a conceptual proposal, is usually no more than five pages long. It is generally provided after one meeting with the client, and contains the following:

1. *Statement of the Problem*   You provide a brief summary setting forth the client's problem. Essentially you outline what you understood the client to say about the situation. Then you state the specific issues, problems, or needs that will be addressed in this preproposal.

2. *Objectives and Major Considerations*   You outline the tasks or goals that need to be accomplished, as you see them. That is, the way you heard the client address what needs to be accomplished. There may be more than one objective. You may need to point out major considerations such as trends in the industry, the political climate, or the availability of personnel.

3. *Methods*   You suggest methods to assist your client in meeting the stated objectives. You specify an action plan that would accomplish each objective.

4. *Qualifications*   You cite your specific qualifications to solve the prospective client's problem. Draw on your experience, skills, accomplishments, specialized education—highlight your unique ability to do the job well.

5. *Costs*   You discuss a framework for a fee structure which would include either an hourly rate or a total project cost. Clarify, however, that costs cannot be fully estimated until a full proposal is developed.

THE ADVANTAGES OF A PRELIMINARY PROPOSAL ARE:

1. It demonstrates to some degree your skills, your ability to relate to the client's needs, and your ability to develop solutions.

2. It provides a mechanism to respond to the frequently asked question, ''Can you give me a proposal on that?'' without requiring a full proposal.

3. It enables you to begin a client relationship. The preproposal will be a basis for further discussion.

4. It gives professionals, especially consultants, a means to demonstrate their competence and capability.

5. It demonstrates the tangibility of your service with specified results.

THE DISADVANTAGES OF PRELIMINARY PROPOSALS ARE:

1. After only one meeting, it might be difficult to respond in enough detail to impress the potential client.

2. It requires time and energy to meet with the client and to prepare the preproposal.

3. Your ideas can be taken and used without compensation.

4. Giving a scaled-down preliminary proposal instead of a full proposal may be perceived as evasive or uncooperative.

A SAMPLE PREPROPOSAL

CONCEPTUAL PROPOSAL FOR THE XYZ TELEVISION SYSTEM PREPARED BY ABC CONSULTING, INC.

Statement of the Problem

- *Background and setting:* The XYZ instructional television system has been successfully broadcasting for the last five years. The mode of instruction has been thoroughly tested. Instructors are proficient in the delivery of courses using live telecasts. The thrust of XYZ has been credit courses in multiple disciplines, with a focus on science courses.

  From all indications, the competition for the tele-instructed students should continue to increase, especially as other institutions make significant investments in video equipment and staff. The window for the introduction and acceptance of tele-instruction may close. This would establish the market share for each local institution as well as those from out of state. But at present the window of opportunity is still wide open. How long this will be the case remains to be seen. Indications are that the market will solidify rapidly, as is usually the case with the introduction of any new product or service.

- *Current situation:* XYZ now wants to increase its market share in order to retire debt. It also wants to continue the growth pattern that has been the hallmark of the program. The mechanism to increase revenues and services is via noncredit courses.

Objectives and Major Considerations

- Market research is now being undertaken by staff. This research should complement the research that has already been conducted on the educational needs of business in the Metro area.

- XYZ should consider becoming more aggressive in its promotional efforts for new clientele. For example, the needs of high-tech industry in the Metro area must be met quickly, else that share of the market will be lost to other institutions, which are becoming much more aggressive.

- Other areas of the state could also be more aggressively approached by XYZ. High-tech companies throughout the state will continue to have acute training needs that can be met by XYZ.

- XYZ programs are still in a growth cycle relative to market share (1,500 enrollments per semester). Credit programs have the greatest potential for growth. Currently there are eighteen companies subscribing, which could be considered an embryonic stage. The market is virtually untapped according to a study we conducted for the Office of Economic Development. In order to stay competitive, high tech companies must have available state-of-the-art training for their staffs.

Methods

In response to the major considerations and objectives outlined above, comprehensive marketing planning is recommended. For maximum impact, it is recommended that all levels of the organization be involved in the planning, since they all contribute to the delivery of programs.

Comprehensive market planning takes into account practical matters. A written plan of action and evaluation program will ensure growth in an increasingly competitive market.

The process of comprehensive market planning includes the following steps.

Step 1: Conduct a marketing audit which assesses the current goals of XYZ, its position in the market, and the involvement of management to ascertain the vision for the programs. In addition, all marketing communications are reviewed as well as the marketing budget and the personnel functions associated with marketing programs. Strengths and weaknesses are identified.

Step 2: Conduct market research to resolve the issues raised in Step 1. Particular attention will be paid to identifying the characteristics of the prospective clientele.

Step 3: Develop a written marketing plan that contains a vision, specific goals, promotional themes, and a communications plan that includes brochures, catalogs, space advertising, and personnel recommendations. Project a budget to achieve the stated goals.

Step 4: Implementation of the marketing plan. Monitor results and track outcomes.

Step 5: Evaluation and fine tuning of activities based on the initial results.

Project Fees

Fees for the project will be estimated once all details of the work are finalized, at which time a more extensive proposal will be provided. The full proposal will contain cost estimates for the complete project.

Qualifications

1. Our firm has completed fifteen successful consulting engagements which involved positioning and promoting nonprofit tele-instructional programs.

2. We possess experience from all relevant organizational levels: faculty, administration, marketing department, and program delivery.

3. We have extensive market research experience for high-tech companies. This has aided in targeting their clientele.

4. We have developed marketing communications campaigns that brought desired results for clients who have a similar organizational profile.

Dated: 2/7/XX

THE SCOPE OF THE WORK (Continued)

FORMAL PROPOSALS

Formal proposals are far more extensive than preproposals. The full proposal is a step-by-step description of what the consultant proposes to do (the work plan), the results that can be expected (the deliverables), the time span, qualifications, and fees.

A proposal is often considered a discussion document that guides both the consultant and the prospective client. It serves as a negotiation tool, with changes or additions coming from both sides.

Once signed and accepted, the proposal essentially becomes an agreement or contract for the work. Proposals are often widely circulated, so they must be well written.

For more information on proposals, see:

1. H. Holtz, *The Consultant's Guide to Proposal Writing*, Wiley, 1986.

2. W. Cohen, *How to Make It Big as a Consultant*, AMACOM, 1985.

3. B. Smith, *The Country Consultant*, Plume, 1982.

4. T. J. Ucko, *Selecting and Working with Consultants*, Crisp, 1990.

CONTRACTS

A contract is an agreement on the work to be done. A clear contract is the foundation of a successful consulting project. As in any relationship, when things go wrong, it's often because of unmet—and usually unexpressed—expectations.

The contract need not be complicated. A letter of agreement outlining what each party will do, and signed by both parties, is often sufficient. But your client's legal or purchasing departments may have more formal contractual requirements, such as nondisclosure agreements, which can add to the complexity of the contract.

The consultant's written proposal often forms the basis for the contract. But clients frequently will add to or amend the proposal in a give-and-take negotiation session. Alternatively, clients may draft letters of agreement or contracts themselves.

WHAT TO INCLUDE IN THE CONTRACT

Here is a list of items that have proven useful in consulting contracts. Check ☑ those items you want to include in your contracts or letters of agreement.

☐ **Term.** When will the agreement take effect? When will it end?

☐ **Objectives.** The results you want to achieve.

☐ **Definition of success.** What is success, and how it it to be measured? Who will do the measuring? When?

☐ **Scope of the project.** Step by step, exactly what tasks and activities will the consultant perform to achieve the desired objectives?

☐ **Deliverable or product.** What will be the result of the consultant's work? A working system? A detailed written report? An oral report? Will there be a formal presentation? When are interim and final reports due? Will you provide ongoing maintenance to a delivered system?

☐ **Ownership of the product.** Sometimes the consultant's product has commercial value, for example, a custom-designed training program. Who will own the copyright? Will the consultant be able to sell the same program to other clients?

☐ **Confidentiality.** Consultants often have access to confidential or proprietary information. If this is the case, you may be asked to agree not to disclose such information to others.

☐ **Communications.** What forms of communication do you want with the client? Periodic phone calls, or meetings? Written progress reports and formal reviews may be required of you.

☐ **Staffing.** Clients want to know who will be working on their project. Are substitutions permitted? Under what circumstances?

☐ **Supervision of the consultant.** To whom will you be responsible and who will be your primary contact?

☐ **Scheduling.** When will the project begin? Are there dates by which interim "milestones" are to be reached? What is the expected completion date?

☐ **Fees and payments.** Will the consultant receive a daily or an hourly rate, a fixed project fee, or a monthly retainer? Will a portion be paid in advance? On a lengthy project, will payments be made at scheduled intervals, or upon achievement of specified interim targets?

☐ **Incentives and penalties.** Will there be financial incentives for the consultant to bring in the project ahead of schedule? Will there be penalties for running late?

☐ **Termination.** What if things don't work out as planned? It's helpful to agree in advance how to end the contract if either party becomes unhappy with the relationship or the progress of the project. How much notice must either party give? What fees will be due?

☐ **Cancellation policy.** What if the project gets canceled before it begins? The consultant may expect compensation for days that have been reserved for the client and cannot easily be "sold" on short notice.

☐ **Arbitration.** If disputes arise over deliverables, fees, or other contract items, how will they be resolved? Often, the parties will agree in advance to refer disputes to the American Arbitration Association or a similar organization for binding arbitration.

(The author is indebted to T. J. Ucko, *Selecting and Working with Consultants*, Crisp Publications, 1990, for material on the consulting contract.)

THE SCOPE OF THE WORK (Continued)

LETTERS OF AGREEMENT

Somewhat informal, a letter of agreement briefly details the nature of the work to be done, the cost, the time schedule, and specific limitations, if any. In addition, terms of payment are also included. Once signed and accepted by both parties, the letter of agreement serves as the contract for the work. But until its acceptance, it is a working document that is usually prepared by the consultant. A sample follows:

February 14, 1991

Ms. Gloria Gold
President
XYZ Corporation
1234 American Ave.
Anytown, USA

LETTER OF AGREEMENT

Dear Ms. Gold,

Thank you for the opportunity to serve as your marketing consultant. As we discussed by phone today, this letter of agreement serves to detail our working relationship. My role will be that of consultant/coach in marketing as you take the lead to develop a comprehensive marketing plan for the seminar program for technical supervisors. I will offer suggestions and react to your initiatives as you develop the plan. However, if we agree, I will undertake certain specific assignments, such as market research. In order to serve you best, I suggest we meet regularly, especially at the beginning of the project.

In order to minimize the cost of travel time, I suggest that our meetings be conducted in my office. However, if it is more convenient or necessary for me to travel from my office, my travel time would be calculated at my hourly fee.

The hourly fee we agreed upon is $99.00. Portions of hours will be charged in quarter-hour increments. All billables must be pre-approved by you. Expenses such as long-distance telephone and copying will be billed separately and in detail. Billable phone calls are charged at my hourly rate, at a minimum charge of one quarter-hour per call. These calls may replace meetings, to use time more efficiently.

Billing will be every two weeks, with terms of payment net thirty days. Please make all checks payable to ABC Consulting, Inc. For your records, my federal tax number is 123-45-6789. Either party may terminate this agreement at any time with two weeks' notice in writing. Compensation for my work will be up to the date of termination.

If these conditions are agreeable to you, please sign the enclosed copy and return it to me. The copy that I have signed is for your records. If you have questions, please do not hesitate to call me. I look forward to working with you.

Sincerely yours,

Joseph James

Joseph James
President, ABC Consulting, Inc.

Accepted and agreed to: _____   _____
                              President, XYZ Corp.   Date

A FINAL WORD ON CONTRACTING & SETTING FEES

Regardless of how the work to be done is contracted (formally or informally), what you are attempting to do as a consultant is communicate effectively with your clients. You are negotiating the work to be done.

After the contract, the trick to effective communication is frequency (e.g., weekly meetings), purpose (e.g., progress reports), and feedback (i.e., just how you are doing as the consultant).

The spirit of the contract is as important as the contract. That is the stuff that cannot be defined in the contract but involves effectively communicating with the boss—your client!

SETTING FEES

Many factors affect the fees that consultants charge. Some of the most common factors are:

- *Reputation*   The fee a consultant can command might well be based on how noted he or she is in the field. The more noted, the more you can charge. Fees are a function of value, and value is a function of reputation in the eyes of prospects.

- *Prevailing Rate*   Sometimes, a daily or hourly standard rate is dictated by tradition within a given field or in a given area of the country.

- *Consultant Role*   A problem solver may command a greater fee than a process consultant whose role is to help install a system or procedures. Consultants' roles vary, and so do fees for the various roles.

- *Value Added*   Fees are based on the results that the consultant expects to achieve and of their worth to the client in real dollars. The consultant's track record and reputation play heavily in this approach.

- *Expenses and Income*   Fees are determined by what the consultant wants or needs to earn. Those new to consulting are often most influenced by what they need to earn to break even, since their reputations have yet to be established.

Consultants new to their field with little reputation generally cannot charge what more accomplished and experienced consultants can charge. However, there are exceptions to everything.

What will affect your fee structure most? Write your answer in the space below.

_____

_____

SETTING FEES (Continued)

Methods of calculating fees generally fall into these categories:

1. *Project fee:* An agreed-upon fixed fee for a defined project is established in advance. The actual time spent by the consultant has no bearing on the fee. The consultant calculates his or her fee by (1) multiplying the hourly billing rate by the estimated time to be spent, or (2) charging what he or she thinks the project is worth to the client.

2. *Time charges:* The consultant multiplies an hourly or daily rate (the billing rate) by the actual number of hours or days spent on the project.

3. *Retainer:* Consultants on retainer receive regular monthly payments. The payments may be in exchange for recurring work, assurance of the consultant's availability, or a discounted billing rate.

Out-of-pocket expenses are usually reimbursed. Many consultants charge for travel time but usually at a reduced rate.

What method of calculating fees will you choose, and why? Write your answer in the space below.

I will choose the _____ method, because

_____

_____

EXAMPLE FEE CALCULATION

To illustrate just how fees are determined, an example of the expenses-and-income approach follows. Most new consultants use this approach, because they don't know what they can command in the market.

Using this method, three major factors are considered:

1. The annual gross income the consultant requires to cover personal living expenses, or simply the net income the consultant would ideally like to make in the year in question.

2. The time available for consulting. This can be thought of as the time available for sale.

3. All business expenses.

Consider this calculation for a one-person consulting firm in the first year of operation.

A desired $60,000 gross income yearly.

There are 2,080 hours available for consulting (40 hours $\times$ 52 weeks).

No other expenses are considered at this point.

Fee calculation: The basic hourly rate is $28.85 ($60,000 divided by 2,080 billable hours).

Now let's look at some other factors to be considered in the fee calculation.

The consultant plans to take two weeks' vacation per year, including holidays (2 $\times$ 40 = 80 hours).

Assume 22 days per year are needed for office administration, such as billing. (8 $\times$ 22 = 176 hours).

The billable hours are therefore reduced to 2,080 − 80 − 176 = 1,824.

Fee calculation: The hourly rate must increase to $32.89 ($60,000 divided by 1,824 billable hours) to reach the desired $60,000.

If the business is to grow, the consultant will need to spend time on marketing.

Business development activities usually require a minimum of 25% of the consultant's time (25% $\times$ 1,824 = 456).

This limits the consulting time available to 1,824 − 456 = 1,368 billable hours.

Fee calculation: The hourly rate increases again, to $43.86 ($60,000 divided by 1,368 hours).

Now let's look at insurance and pension expenses.

Health insurance: $2,400; life insurance: $2,000; disability insurance: $1,500; FICA: $5,500; liability insurance: $500; car insurance: $500. Total: $12,400 per year.

For the consultant to receive net earning of $60,000, his gross earning must be $60,000 + $12,400 = $72,400.

Fee calculation: The hourly billing rate increases to $52.92 ($72,400 divided by 1,368 hours).

SETTING FEES (Continued)

At this point, we need to consider all the other business expenses and overhead that the consultant will incur each year.

Supplies: $500

Printing of cards, stationery, etc.: $1,500

Utilities: $1,000

Telephone equipment and service: $1,500

Postage: $500

Office equipment—copier, fax, computer: $8,000

Car repairs and gas: $2,500

Parking: $200

Entertainment: $500

Rent ($600 monthly): $7,200

Promotion: $2,000

Dues to professional associations: $1,200

Travel to professional meetings: $1,000

Training: $500

Accountant: $500

Legal fees: $500

The total yearly business and overhead expenses come to *approximately* $29,100.

Fee calculation: The hourly billing rate must increase to $74.19 ($72,400 + $29,100 = $101,500, divided by 1,368 hours).

Rarely is a consultant able to sell or work every available billable hour, in this case 1,368. This is due to scheduling complexity—you aren't available when the client needs you, or you are available when clients do not need you. Or all the billable time may not be sold. Unsold hours are known as downtime. It can be used for something else, especially marketing. But unfortunately it is not billable time.

A realistic allowance for downtime is 25% of the billable hours. 1,368 × 75% = 1,026 billable hours. The yearly billable hours are now down from the original 2,080 to 1,026—a 50% reduction! This translates to 128 days of billable work, if your orientation is to days rather than hours.

Final fee calculation: The hourly rate becomes $99.00 ($101,500 divided by 1,026 billable hours). A $792 daily rate ($99 × 8 hours) is required to achieve the financial goal of $60,000 gross income yearly.

NOW YOU TRY IT

Calculate your own fees. It will give you the ability to answer the question, ''What should I charge for my fees?'' Better yet, it will give you the ability to explain to prospective clients why you charge such outrageous fees! Quite the contrary. As you can see from the example above, consultants—experts in their field—really don't charge that much when you consider their expenses and the income a consultant merits.

MAKING THE CLIENT HAPPY

The relationship that you begin to establish during the first meeting becomes more solidified each step of the way—from the unknown prospect to the client you work closely with.

Each client represents a relationship, and is also another boss. The consultant has many bosses—clients—that must be satisfied. That's why it's so important to consider how client relationships are managed.

Each relationship is influenced by both the consultant and the client. Here we address what the consultant can do to impact the relationship—to make the client happy.

1. Provide regular progress reports so there are no surprises at the end of the assignment. Clients deserve to be well informed about your work's status at all times.

2. Avoid internal politics. Your client has to deal with organizational politics and does not want you to get involved. That would make his or her life more complicated. So avoid internal issues like a plague.

3. Emphasize the benefits of your work at all times. Clients are busy, and they often forget the value of the work you are doing. Note the benefits of the work in tangible terms as frequently as possible.

4. Define what you mean by quality work as frequently as possible. Defining quality outcomes gives you some degree of control over the work.

5. Establish channels of communication with everyone involved in your work. Where appropriate, schedule regular meetings, provide written progress reports, have frequent phone conversations, and take notes, regardless of the communication channel. An effective consultant is a great communicator!

6. Discuss small problems before they become major problems. Stay on top of the job and it won't get the best of you.

7. Be prepared to deal with delays caused by the client that impair your ability to meet deadlines. Be extremely sensitive to deadlines and what is in the way of meeting them. Inform your client early about what is getting in the way.

8. Provide bills that give sufficient information so that your client can easily approve them and get you paid on time.

9. Put yourself in the client's shoes at all times. Know your clients and you will know what makes them happy!

ACTION PLANNING GUIDE

To help you keep your momentum, the following guide encourages you to take action. Remember, the best laid plans are the ones that get implemented! Write your answers in the spaces provided.

1. The very next step I need to take is:

_____

_____

2. The area that needs the most development for me to become a consultant is:

_____

I plan to develop this area by:

_____

_____

3. After reading this book, I have decided whether or not consulting is not for me. My decision is:

_____

My reasons for this decision are:

_____

_____

4. Using the bibliography that follows, I want to further explore the following topics:

_____

_____

_____

5. The most important thing I have learned about myself by reading this book is:

_____

_____

_____

BIBLIOGRAPHY

Alston, F. M. *Contracting with the Federal Government*. Wiley, 1989.

Barcus, S. W. and J. W. Wilkinson, editors. *Handbook of Management Consulting Services*. McGraw-Hill, 1989.

Bermont, H.I. *The Complete Consultant: A Roadmap to Success*. Consultant's Library, 1982.

Blake, R. R. *Consultation: A Handbook for Individual and Organization Development*. Addison-Wesley, 1983.

Cohen, W. *How to Make It Big as a Consultant*. AMACOM, 1985.

Connor, R. A., and J. P. Davidson. *Marketing Your Consulting and Professional Services*. Wiley, 1985.

_____. *Getting New Clients*. Wiley, 1987.

Courtney, T. W., and K. J. Thomas. *The Guide to High-Tech Consulting and Contracting*. Madden, 1987.

Creedy, R. F., *Time Is Money*. Dutton, 1980.

_____. *Steps to Professional Independence: A Guide to Packaging, Pricing, and Selling Your Skills*. Madison, 1988.

Golightly, H. O. *Consultants: Selecting, Using and Evaluating Business Consultants*. Watts, 1985.

Greenbaum, T. L. *The Consultant's Manual*. Wiley, 1989.

Greenfield, W. M. *Successful Management Consulting*. Prentice-Hall, 1987.

Greiner, L. E., and R. O. Metzger. *Consulting to Management*. Prentice-Hall, 1983.

Holtz, H. *How to Succeed as an Independent Consultant*. Wiley, 1983.

_____. *Successful Newsletter Publishing for the Consultant*. Consultant's Library, 1983.

_____. *The Consultant's Edge: Using the Computer as a Marketing Tool*. Wiley, 1985.

_____. *Utilizing Consultants Successfully: A Guide for Management in Business*. Quorum, 1985.

_____. *Advice, A High Profit Business: A Guide for Consultants and Other Entrepreneurs*. Prentice-Hall, 1986.

_____. *Consultant's Guide to Proposal Writing*. Wiley, 1986.

_____. *Expanding Your Consulting Practice With Seminars*. Wiley, 1987.

_____. *The Consultant's Guide to Winning Clients*. Wiley, 1988.

Karlson, D. *Marketing Your Consulting or Professional Services*. Crisp, 1988.

92

Kelley, R. E. *The Complete Guide to a Profitable Career*. Scribner, 1986.

Kemppainen, R. C. *Power Consulting: Using the Media to Expand Your Business*. Wiley, 1988.

Klein, C. *Consultants Reference Guide*. Scarecrow, 1989.

Kotler, P. and P. N. Bloom. *Marketing Professional Services*. Prentice-Hall, 1984.

Lant, J. *Money Talks: The Complete Guide to Creating a Profitable Workshop or Seminar in Any Field*. JLA, 1985.

Martin, C. *Starting Your New Business*. Crisp, 1988.

Nevis, E. C. *Organizational Consulting: A Gestalt Approach*. Gardner, 1987.

Phillips, K. *A Consultancy Approach for Trainers*. University Associates, 1989.

Pickens, J. E. *The Freelancer's Handbook: A Comprehensive Guide to Selling Your Freelance Services*. Prentice-Hall, 1981.

Shenson, H. L. *The Contract and Fee-Setting Guide for Consultants and Professionals*. Wiley, 1989.

Smith, B. *The Country Consultant*. Plume, 1982.

Stryker, S. C. *Principles; and Practices of Professional Consulting*. Consultant's Library, 1982.

_____. *Guide to Successful Consulting*. Prentice-Hall, 1984.

Tepper, R. *Become a Top Consultant*. Wiley, 1985.

_____. *The Consultant's Problem-Solving Workbook*. Wiley, 1987.

Weinberg, G. *The Secrets of Consulting: A Guide to Giving and Getting Advice Successfully*. Dorset, 1985.

NOTES

FOR OTHER FIFTY-MINUTE SELF-STUDY BOOKS
SEE THE BACK OF THIS BOOK.

NOTES

FOR OTHER FIFTY-MINUTE SELF-STUDY BOOKS
SEE THE BACK OF THIS BOOK.

We hope you enjoyed this book. If so, we have good news for you. This title is part of the best-selling *FIFTY-MINUTE*™ *Series* of books. All *Series* books are similar in size and identical in price. Several are supported with training videos (identified by the symbol Ⓥ next to the title).

FIFTY-MINUTE Books and Videos are available from your distributor. A free catalog is available upon request from Crisp Publications, Inc., 1200 Hamilton Court, Menlo Park, California 94025.

FIFTY-MINUTE Series Books & Videos organized by general subject area.

Management Training:

Small Business & Financial Planning:

Adult Literacy & Learning:

Career/Retirement & Life Planning: